SPEAK...

S A Y...

PRAY...

BRENDA JOYCE MILLS

Speak, SAY, Pray

Copyright © September 2023 by Brenda J. Mills

ISBN (978-17345305-8-2)

Printed in USA by 48HrBooks www.48HrBooks.com

WORD(S) DEFINITIONS:
Thorndike Barnhart Dictionary, ScottForesman

BIBLICAL SCRIPTURES:
King James Version

COMPLEMENTARY PRAYERS AND
SCRIPTURES:

Brother Larry J. Johnson, I, Teacher Destini J. Stephens, Elder Crystal Stephens, Deacon Tony L. Mills, Sr.

A SPECIAL THANKS TO:

Samonza Kimble, Larry J. Johnson II, Kimberly Johnson

www.Kingdommindedwriters.com

brenskingdommindedwriters@gmail.com

313.683.3119

PRAYER
Pray, Praying, Prays

Communicating with Father GOD

Acknowledging GOD
Asking GOD to Help You
Asking GOD to Guide You
Petitioning GOD to Agree with You
Just telling GOD Thank You

A COMPONENT OF FAITH IS:
"Believing that, it can and shall happen."

TABLE OF CONTENTS

Affirmations, Confessions & Prayers Defined 7

Dedication 8

Preface 10

Introduction Who GOD Is 14

Chapter 1 GOD At A Glance 15

Chapter 2 Right Words, Positive Vibes 29

Chapter 3 Affirmations 41

Chapter 4 Wrong Words, Negative Vibes 50

Chapter 5 Binding & Loosing Confessions 62

Chapter 6 Biblical Prayers 91

Chapter 7 Heartfelt Prayers 113

Chapter 8 Totally Trusting GOD 142

Chapter 9 Motivate, Inspire, Nudge 147

Chapter 10 Names of GOD and Prayers 161

Chapter 11 Conclusion 168

There will be times when situations, atmospheres and things will become uncomfortable and rough, because the enemy(satan) is busy trying to discourage, kill, steal and destroy us, GOD's children.

And yes, it's ideal and always good for people to pray for others, especially for those who we personally love and care about. But we also need to know how to pray and make affirmations for ourselves, because we don't know the course of someone's day. They may not have an opportunity to include us in their prayers.

That's why it's important to make time and speak words of life, through prayers, affirmations, and confessions regarding one's self daily or as much as possible.

Affirmations (Affirm): Declare positively to be true; maintain firmly; assert; confirm or ratify. A positive statement; a solemn declaration have the legal force of an oath, and made by persons whose religion or conscience forbids the taking of an oath.

Confessions: An owning up; acknowledgment; admission; acknowledged of belief; profession of faith; belief acknowledged; creed; person who acknowledges belief (confessor)

Pray: Speak to GOD in worship; enter into spiritual communion with GOD; offer worship. Make earnest request to GOD or to any other object of worship. Ask earnestly; implore; beseech (*pray to GOD for help*).

Prayer: act of praying. Thing prayed for. Form of words to be used in praying. form of worship; religious service consisting mainly of prayers. An earnest or humble request. (chance of success: *the plan never had a prayer.*)

DEDICATION

This book is dedicated to whomsoever will believe Father GOD, LORD Jesus and The Holy Spirit. And pick up their cross *(putting aside our selfish thoughts, forsake worldly ways and yield to righteousness, GOD)* and follow Jesus. It's not about what we think or say, but what does the bible say about the matters.

Then said they unto him, Lord, evermore give us this bread. And Jesus said unto them, I am the bread of life: he that cometh to me shall never hunger; and he that believeth on me shall never thirst. John 6:35

And this is the will of him that sent me, that everyone which seeth the Son, and believeth on him, may have everlasting life: and I will raise him up at the last day. John 6:40

Verily, verily, I say unto you, He that believeth on me hath everlasting life. I am the bread of life.

John 6:47-48

I am the living bread which came down from heaven: if any man eat of this bread, he shall live for ever: and the bread that I will give is my flesh, which I will give for the life of the world.   John 6:51

It is the spirit that quickeneth; the flesh profiteth nothing: the words that I speak unto you, *they* are spirit, and they are life.   John 6:63-65

The grass withereth, the flower fadeth: but the word of our GOD shall stand forever.   Isaiah 40:8

The words of the LORD are pure words: as silver tried in a furnace of earth, purified seven times.
(pin note: whatever you're hoping, praying and believing GOD for; put faith (action) towards it at least seven times)
Psalms 12:6

Sanctify them through thy truth: thy word is truth.
John 17:17

For the word of the LORD is right; and all his works are done in truth.   Psalms 33:4

PREFACE

Our hearts can sometimes become tremendously encouraged, through one scripture, one word in a scripture, or a word from someone on our path. That interacting can channel an answer of hope, remove a splinter like irritation, or lead us towards an open door to something beautifully needful that has been sent to us because of GOD's unfailing and never-ending love for us.

This book *"Speak, SAY, Pray"* was inspired from me leisurely reading *Luke 17:1-5*. Jesus's disciples asked him to increase their faith. And though I had read *Luke 17:1-5* many times before, it was during an unexpected moment that the word, **"SAY"** in the scripture became billboard magnified and immediately registered in my mind like never before. I suddenly felt very excited, enlightened, and relieved. It was like I had been searching for something and it finally appeared. I hadn't connected faith with **saying** something, I thought faith was mainly believing, hoping, and waiting for something to happen.

I have benefited greatly from the word **"Say"** in *Luke 17:5*. It has compelled me to speak my desired outcomes into situations and experiences. It has resulted and rewarded me with victories in many areas of my life. I now know and understand that if I am not pleased with a situation, I can **say** something to change it. And if things are going well, I can **say** something to keep it going. I know how to exchange what's dimed, doomed and mentally unhealthy to having, hope, and Yes Lord, Thank You Jesus moments by what I **say**.

The revelation of the word **"Say"** has since caused me to overcome negative health and financial issues. A couple of years ago I began having excruciating uncomfortable pain in one of my legs. I went to a couple of doctors *(one of them suggested surgery)* and tried various ways to make the pain go away without having surgery. The diagnosis was, I had a "baker cyst" a term and medical issue I had never heard of. And finally, months later while I'm still experiencing pain and moving at a slower physical pace, the Holy Spirit said, put a word on it, **say** something. So, I began speaking the *bind and loose principles*, and immediately, the next day, the physical issue became better, my pain had decreased in stature, roughly eighty-seven percent without me having surgery. And I no longer needed long term medication, only the one prescription for pain during the early stages of the health issue.

The revelation knowledge of the word "**SAY**" additionally came during a time when I was unmarried, financially struggling in some areas and had a credit card debt that wouldn't go away. So, I began **saying** scriptures while attentively listening, to GOD, Lord Jesus, and the Holy Spirit, to acquire answers that would allow me to have a better and more productive life. I desired to feel good physically, mentally, and be financially fit. I needed to change and incorporate in my life the things that would give and leave me with positive, more permanent, long-lasting results regarding my mental, physical, and financial wellbeing.

Today, I can say that the word "**SAY**" has increased my faith, renewed my thought process, changed my vocabulary, to a better way of thinking and living.

And from that point of time until now *(eternity)*, I truly believe that **saying** something is a key to the doors that will usher us in to a brighter, more positive, and prosperous way of living. And today, I can say all is well, and I'm very grateful to Father GOD for calling me out of darkness and into His marvelous light.

The LORD has elevated my faith, endowed me with wisdom, revelation knowledge and an understanding through one word, **"SAY"**, and again, I'm very grateful. I truly believe that spiritually seeing and hearing the word **"SAY"** during that particular moment was, intimacy and favour with the LORD and divinely timed.

> *"Then they cry unto the LORD in their trouble, He saveth them out of their distresses. He sent his word, and healed them, and delivered them from their destructions. Oh that men would praise the Lord for his goodness, and for his wonderful works to the children of men".* Psalms 107:19-21

INTRODUCTION

GOD is great, enormously big, very good and all knowing. **He's OMNIPOTENT**, *(having all power; almighty, having very great power, or influence)* that He can answer a prayer request, make a confession come to fruition, any place, time, and way He chooses.

He's OMNIPRESENCE, *(present everywhere at the same time)*. No man on Earth has the monopoly and know exactly who, what, when and how GOD will bless and bring someone's prayers, affirmations, confessions and thoughts into existence.

He's so **OMNISCIENCE**, *(knowledge of everything; complete or infinite knowledge)* that He created everyone with their own set of fingerprints. When I think about the trillions of people who have been born into this world and no two individuals have the same set of fingerprints, all I can think and say is, GOD is such an Amazingly Phenomenal GOD.

CHAPTER 1 ONE

G O D At A Glance

The Bible is the authentic voice of GOD and His historical relationships with man. We're so blessed to have a blueprint, instructions, and history about GOD, man, demographics, relationships, and the many phases of life that have taken place from the beginning of time unto now.

Reading and learning who GOD is through the bible gives us an opportunity to personally know exactly who GOD is from the spirit of GOD; and not solely by what we've heard through ministers and others. The Bible tells us what is pleasing to Father GOD and what is not acceptable to Him.

The bible is loaded with history, various experiences, stories, and examples. History pushes and helps us to move forward. Experience informs us about the mistakes and errors that others may have encountered. Stories and examples present facts pertaining to how people lived, what they believed, and the possibilities that comes with life when GOD is included in our daily lives; what was beneficial and what was not. We mature, our faith increases when we know, have an understanding about the pros, cons, and outcomes of various situations. Faith comes by hearing, and hearing by the **"word"** of GOD, *Romans 10:17*.

The bible also says and show us that GOD is no respector of persons, and if He did something for one, He'll do it for another regardless of our title, background, mistakes, gender, race, and age, we only need to ask Him. And if we don't read the bible or hear the preacher, we won't know what to ask, nor what to expect.

The bible has shown us through the various stories within its context, that we can ask *(pray to GOD)* about anything or **say** specific words and get results from our prayers, confessions, affirmations, and the bind and loose principles. And there have also been instances when some people have passionately thought about some things, uttered nothing, yet those very things that were thought about, produced positive results, to what was being mentally hoped for. That's being connected to GOD.

And today, it's good to know that GOD's way of operating and doing things hasn't changed. What He said in His **"word"** when He first created the world and man, applies now as well, the only difference is, man has changed. One generation is gone, and another is born to activate, experience GOD's instructions, laws, judgement, statues, and principles. GOD's order of operation and cycle will continue. There's nothing new under the sun, the next generation will freshly experience and learn GOD's methods of operating as well as the generations to come.

GOD desires that we know who He is and the miraculous and wonderful things He has done for us. He's hoping that we praise Him for His goodness; for His wonderful works towards those who are called His children, and those who follow His Son, Jesus. He wants us to respect, reverence and freely worship and love Him, the way He loves us, unconditionally forever. He desires that our relationship with Him be sound and trusting.

"Verily I say unto you, This generation shall not pass, till all these things be fulfilled. Heaven and earth shall pass away, but my __words__ shall not pass away".

Matthew 24:34-35

GOD's CREATIONS

GOD created the World, with both words and His hands. GOD spoke, then He formed and created something in the physical. Everything that GOD created has movement and is full of life. From mankind, the fishes in the seas, fowls in the air, the two, four and eight legged creatures on land, flowers, plants, trees, air, the sky, clouds, dirt, grass, and weeds exist because of what GOD said and did.

Words can cause something to be birthed, cause something to exist or make something nil and void, GOD's creations produce after their own kind and fails not. *"In the beginning GOD created the heaven and the earth. And the earth was without form, and void; and darkness was upon the face of the deep. And the Spirit of GOD moved upon the face of the waters. And **<u>GOD said</u>**, Let there be light: and there was light. And GOD saw the light, that it was good: and GOD divided the light from the darkness. And **GOD called** the light Day, and the darkness he called Night. And the evening and the morning were the first day. And **<u>GOD said</u>**, Let there be a firmament in the* midst of the waters, and let it divide the waters from the waters. And GOD made the firmament, and divided the waters which were under the firmament from the waters which were above the firmament: and it was so. And **GOD called** the firmament Heaven. And the evening and the morning were the second day. And **GOD said**, Let the waters under the heaven be gathered together unto one place, and let the dry land appear: and it was so. And **GOD called** the dry land Earth; and the gathering together of the waters called he Seas: and GOD saw that it was good. And **GOD said**, Let the earth bring forth grass, the herb yielding seed, and the fruit tree yielding fruit after his kind, whose seed is in itself, upon the earth: and it was so. And the earth brought forth grass, and herb yielding seed after his kind, and the tree yielding fruit, whose seed was in itself, after his kind: and GOD saw that it was good. And the evening and the morning were the third day. And **GOD said**, Let there be lights in the firmament of the heaven to divide the day from the night; and let them be for signs, and for seasons, and for days, and years". Genesis 1:1-14

The **"word"** of GOD also says that mankind is created in GOD's image, which means we will have some of GOD's attributes, to say, create and make things as well. The same way we have attributes and ways like our natural parents and our children after us.

We're not exactly like our parents, and our children are not exactly like us, but there are many similarities. And each moment that we're spending time with someone, we're learning from them. We're putting into action what we have been taught and seen. Spending time reading the bible, will cause us to behave and have some results like GOD, which will also position us to become who GOD desires us to be. *"And GOD said, Let us make man in our image, after our likeness: and let them have dominion over the fish of the sea, and over the fowl of the air; and over the cattle, and over all the earth, and over every creeping thing that creepeth upon the earth. So, GOD created man in his own image, in the image of GOD created he him; male and female created he them"*. *Genesis 1:26-27*

GOD'S INSTRUCTIONS

In *Genesis 2:20,* GOD told Adam to give names to the animals on land, fish of the sea, and fowls in the air, and Adam did as GOD had instructed him, with little effort because Adam had many attributes and qualities like GOD the one who created him.

GOD created man and verbally communicated with man as needed. GOD also told Adam in Genesis how to take care of the Garden of Eden. GOD told Moses and his brother Aaron in the book of Exodus how to deliver and lead the people from the hardships of Egypt. GOD additionally instructed Moses and Aaron where to build a tabernacle, what size to make it, what to put in the tabernacle; along with the days and time to worship Him in the tabernacle. In the book of Leviticus, GOD also tells man what kind of meat and fish to eat.

Everything that GOD created, had instructions attached to them, as objects and things do today, especially something new. GOD gave darkness, light, water, and land instructions. He told them when to be sullen, when to shine, how far to expand and when to stay put.

Instructions help and allow us to have a better, easier way of doing something. Automobiles, home appliances, cooking, clothing, technology, schools, driving, swimming, sporting events have some form of instructions attached to them. And when we're not feeling well, we seek a doctor to learn what's wrong; and in return the doctor gives us instructions that will heal or help us get better.

GOD's instructions will allow us to have opportunities for a prosperous, peaceable, lengthy, and not always perfect, but pleasing lifestyle. Our mental, physical wellbeing and relationships will be gratifying. Our walks of life will be smooth and the scenery beautiful when we follow the instructions, of GOD the one who created us. There are many wonderful benefits that comes with being saved, born again, having a renewed mind, and serving GOD.

Even if someone is not born again, nor exercise and execute GOD's **"word"** on a regular basis; GOD's principles and methods of operating will still give them positive effects and keep them afloat. *"So shall my word be that goeth forth out of my mouth: it shall not return unto me void, but it shall accomplish that which I please, and it shall prosper in the thing whereto I sent it." Isaiah 55:11*.

One of the best benefits to being connected and living for GOD is knowing that His personality and methods of operation are the same daily. And that GOD doesn't love and judge us by our looks; what we're wearing and the possessions we have accumulated. He is righteous, merciful, gracious, just, grudgeless, and always willing to forgive us, of our errors, mistakes, and sin if we ask Him.

GOD wants us to acknowledge, appreciate and willingly love Him the same way we want people to love us. GOD desires that we keep His ten commandments and believe in His Only Begotten Son, Christ Jesus, who is Our Saviour, Our Redeemer, Our Hope and Whoever we need Him to be.

THE TEN COMMANDMENTS
Exodus 20:1-17

1) *Thou shalt have no other gods before me.*

2) *Thou shalt not make unto thee any graven image, or any likeness of anything that is in heaven above, or that is in the earth beneath, or that is in the water under the earth. Thou shalt not bow down thyself to them, nor serve them: for I the Lord thy God am a jealous God.*

3) *Thou shalt not take the name of the Lord thy God in vain.*

4) *Remember the Sabbath day, to keep it holy.*

5) *Honor thy father and thy mother: that thy days may be long upon the land.*

6) *Thou shalt not kill.*

7) *Thou shalt not commit adultery.*

8) *Thou shalt not steal.*

9) *Thou shalt not bear false witness against thy neighbor.*

10) *Thou shall not covet thy neighbour's house, wife, manservant, maidservant, not any thing that is thy neighbour's property.*

VARIOUS METHODS TO HOW GOD RESPOND'S REGARDING THE WORDS WE SAY

GOD has various ways to make our affirmations, confession, prayers, bind and loose principles come to fruition. *GOD can and may*:

- immediately make our confession, come to fruition. *"And Jesus stood, and commanded him to be brought unto him: and when he was come near, he asked him, Saying What wilt thou that I shall do unto thee? And he said, Lord, that I may receive my sight. And Jesus said unto him, Receive thy sight: thy faith hath saved thee. And <u>immediately</u> he received his sight, and followed him, glorifying GOD: and all the people, when they saw it, gave praise unto GOD."* Luke 18:40-43

- show us what actions to take regarding our confessions, affirmations, and prayers.

- give instructions, directions to what is being confessed and affirmed.

- tell us what's wrong and what needs to be done, to be rid of the negative.

- or how to usher in the positive.
- GOD loves us so much that He will occasionally prevent an affirmation or confession from coming to pass; because He knows what we're saying is not a good fit for us. GOD knows our worth, and He desires something more meaningful and special for us. *"For I know the thoughts that I thank towards you, saith the LORD, thoughts of peace, and not of evil, to give you an expected end. Then shall ye call upon me, and ye shall go and pray unto me, and I will hearken unto you. And ye shall seek me, and find me, when ye shall search for me with all your heart."* Jeremiah 29:11-13
- GOD is very gracious that HE will eventually allow us to see and understand why that prayer, affirmation and/or confession did not come to fruition.
- GOD will give us peace, an understanding about a situation, to keep us from spending too much time dwelling on something that's out of our control and is not our battle.
- GOD is also looking at our obedience. If the Holy Spirit whispers or someone else give us instructions to do something regarding what we've been

saying, and we don't apply some form of action, carry out the instructions, then it's very likely that GOD probably won't tell us the next move, towards bringing forth what we're hoping and desire to happen.

When the LORD hears, sees our faith and us taking the time to fellowship with Him *(by reading the bible)* pondering our thoughts before actions, choosing His **"word"** over our emotions, praying, speaking affirmations, and confessing words, He will without doubt manifest those things in our lives. There are benefits that follow the process of faith. Believing, motioning your mouth to speak, say and pray will reward us with the needful things of life and more.

"But without faith it is impossible to please him: for he that cometh to GOD must believe that He is, and that He is a rewarder of them that diligently seek him." Hebrews 11:6

RIGHT WORDS

Our words can bring damage or blessings of life to us and others. "Death and life are in the power of the tongue: and they that love it shall eat the fruit thereof. Proverbs 18:21"

The right words can bring us healings, peace and encouragement. It doesn't matter who said the right words, but it does matter what words were spoken.

POSTIVE VIBES

Let's be attentively wise and not put limits to what GOD would like to do for us, because of the things we say. Concentrate on saying words and phrases that are pretty, as well as encouraging about ourselves and others. The "**word**" says that all things are possible if we believe in GOD. And that we can call those things that be not as though they were. Being positive and putting forth our best efforts daily towards saying, living, and trusting how Jesus, (GOD's Only Begotten Son), says man shall live, *(Matthew – Acts & Revelations)* is a goal we should regularly strive for.

Being open to the things of the kingdom of heaven (the "**word**" of GOD) will cause our faith, beliefs and life mature into a prosperous everlasting joy. *"And Jesus looking upon them saith, With men it is impossible, but not with GOD: for with GOD all things are possible."* Mark 10:27. *"(As it is written, I have made thee a father of many nations,) before him whom he believed, even GOD who quickenenth the dead, and calleth those things which be not as though they were."* Romans 4:17

THE RIGHT WORDS

Praying, affirming, confessing, saying the **right words** creates atmospheres to bring hope, dreams, life expectations and faith to fruition.

The right words can and will:

- make someone feel good
- bring about smiles, bring about healings
- cause someone to be healed and restored
- open the heart to forgive
- will compel others to give unto you
- cause someone to fall in love
- compel and make someone rich and wealthy
- break a curse
- make someone victorious
- give and prepare us for promotions
- cause us to be financially prosperous
- bring peace and cause someone to have mental peace
- cause a person to dwell in peaceable habitations
- bring and allow us to have friends
- give us favor with both, GOD and man

The following are **W**ords *scripturally based* that can be prayed, confessed, and affirmed. Words with benefits that will bless, open doors of opportunities to someone who understands the importance of saying the right words. And who chooses to **say** and do what's rightly correct.

Deliver me from the enemy's hand? Or, Redeem me from the hand of the mighty? Teach me, and **I will hold my tongue**: and cause me to understand wherein I have erred. how forcible are the right words.   Job 6:23-25

As GOD liveth, who hath taken away my judgement; and the Almighty, who hath vexed my soul; All the while my breath is in me, and the spirit of GOD is in my nostrils; **My lips shall not speak wickedness, nor my togue utter deceit.** GOD forbid that I should justify you: till I die I will not remove my integrity from me. My righteousness I hold fast, and will not let it go: my heart shall not reproach me so long as I live.   Job 27:2-6

Thou shalt also **decree a thing**, and it shall be established unto thee: and the light shall shine upon thy ways.
Job 22:28

My heart is inditing a good matter: I speak of the things which I have made touching the king: **my tongue is the pen of a ready writer**.   Psalms 45:1

The **mouth of a righteous *man is* a well of life**: but violence covereth the mouth of the wicked. Hatred stirreth up strifes: but love covereth all sins. **In the lips of him that** __hath understanding wisdom is found__: but a rod *is* for the back of him that is void of understanding.   Proverbs 10:13

I shall not die, but live, and **declare** the works of the LORD.
                                                    Psalms 118:17

Thy **word *is* a lamp unto my feet, and a light unto my path.** I have sworn, and I will perform *it*, that I will keep thy righteous judgments.   Psalms 119:105

The **wicked is snared by the transgression of his lips**: but the just shall come out of trouble.   Proverbs 12:13

A man shall **be satisfied with good by the fruit of his mouth**: and the recompence of a man's hands shall be rendered unto him.   Proverbs 12:14

There is that speaketh like the piercings of a sword: **but the tongue of the wise is health**. The lip of truth shall be established for ever: but a lying tongue is but for a moment.   Proverbs 12:18-19

Heaviness in the heart of man maketh it stoop: but **a good word maketh it glad**.   Proverbs 12:25

A **man shall eat good by the fruit of his mouth**: but the soul of the transgressors shall eat violence. He that **keepeth his mouth keepeth his life**: but he that openeth wide his lips shall have destruction.   Proverbs 13:2-3

A soft answer turneth away wrath: but grievous words stir up anger. The **tongue of the wise** useth knowledge aright: but the **mouth of fools** poureth out foolishness.
Proverbs 15:1-2

The **lips of the wise disperse knowledge**: but the heart of the foolish doeth not so.   Proverbs 15:7

A **man hath joy by the answer of his mouth**: and a **word *spoken*** in due season, how good *is it*! The way of life *is* above to the wise, that he may depart from hell beneath.   Proverbs 15:23-24

The thoughts of the wicked *are* an abomination to the LORD: but **the words of the pure *are* pleasant words**.
Proverbs 15:26

A **man shall be satisfied with good by the fruit of his mouth**: and the recompence of a man's hands shall be rendered unto him.   Proverbs 12:14

Even a fool, when he holdeth his peace, is counted wise: and **he that shutteth his lips** is esteemed a man of understanding.   Proverbs 17:28

The **words of a man's mouth are as deep waters**, and the wellspring of wisdom as a flowing brook.   Proverbs 18:4

A **man's belly shall be satisfied with the fruit of his mouth;** and **with the increase of his lips** shall he be filled.
Proverbs 18:20

Death and life are in **the power of the tongue**: and they that love it shall eat the fruit thereof.   Proverbs 18:21

Whoso **keepeth his mouth** and his tongue **keepeth his soul from trouble**.   Proverbs 21:23

Jesus answered and said unto them, Verily I say unto you, **If ye have faith, and doubt not**, ye shall not only do this which is done to the fig tree, but also **if ye shall say unto this mountain, Be thou removed**, **and be thou cast into the sea; it shall be done**.   Matthew 21:21

For verily I say unto you, That whosoever shall **say** unto this **mountain**, Be thou removed, and be thou **cast into the sea**; and shall not doubt in his heart, but shall believe that those things **which he saith shall come to pass**; **he shall have whatsoever he saith**.   Mark 11:23

And the apostles said unto the Lord, Increase our faith. And the Lord said, **If ye had faith as a grain of mustard seed, ye might say** unto this sycamine tree, Be thou plucked up by the root, and be thou planted in the sea; **and it should obey you**.   Luke 17:5-6

(As it is written, I have made thee a father of many nations,) before him whom he believed, even GOD, who quickeneth the dead, and **calleth those things which be not as though they were**.   Romans 4:17

Therefore I say unto **you**, What things soever ye, desire, **when ye pray**, **believe that ye receive them, and ye shall have them**. And when ye stand **praying,** forgive, if ye have ought against any: that your Father also which is in heaven may forgive you your trespasses.   Mark 11:23-25

This is the third time I am coming to you. **In the mouth** of **two or three** witnesses **shall every word be established**.

2 Corinthians 13:1

Henceforth I call you not servants; for the servant knoweth not what his Lord doeth: but I have called you friends; for all things that I have heard of my Father I have made known unto you. Ye have not chosen me, but I have chosen you, and ordained you, that ye should go and bring forth fruit, and *that* your fruit should remain: **that whatsoever ye shall ask of the Father in my name, he may give it you.** These things I command you, that ye love one another.   John 15:15-17

I am the vine, ye *are* the branches: He that abideth in me, and I in him, the same bringeth forth much fruit: for without me ye can do nothing. If a man abide not in me, he is cast forth as a branch, and is withered; and men gather them, and cast them into the fire, and they are burned. **If ye abide in me, and my words abide in you, ye shall ask what ye will, and it shall be done unto you.**

John 15:5-7

The LORD GOD hasth given **me the tongue of the learned, that I should know how to speak a word in season** to him that is weary: he wakeneth morning by morning, he wakeneth mine ear to hear as the learned. The LORD GOD hath opened mine ear, and I was not rebellious, neither turned away back.   Isaiah 50:4-5

Hear this, all ye people; give ear, all ye inhabitants of the world: Both low and high, rich and poor, together. **My mouth shall speak of wisdom**; and the meditation of my heart shall be of understanding.   Psalms 49:1-3

Wherefore, Job, I pray thee, hear my speeches, and hearken to all my words. **Behold, now I have opened my mouth, my tongue hath spoken in my mouth. My words shall be of the uprightness of my heart: and my lips shall utter knowledge clearly.** The Spirit of GOD hath made me, and the breath of the Almighty hath given me life. If thou canst answer me, set thy words in order before me, stand up.   Job 33:2-5

I have refrained my feet from every evil way, that I might keep thy word. I have not departed from thy judgments: for thou hast taught me. How **sweet are thy words unto my taste**! yea, **sweeter than honey to my mouth**! Through thy precepts I get understanding: therefore I hate every false way. Thy **word is a lamp unto my feet, and a light unto my path.** I have sworn, and I will perform it, that I will keep thy righteous judgments.   Psalms 119:101-105

CHAPTER 3 THREE

AFFIRMATIONS (AFFIRM)

Declare positively to be true; maintain firmly; assert; confirm or ratify. A positive statement; assertion. Confirmation and ratification. Stating that a fact is so. Positive in manner. A word or statement that says yes, agrees.

Believing, hoping and calling those things that be not, as though they were. *Romans 7:14* It is so, and shall be.

AFFIRMATIONS
HEALTHY SELF-ESTEEM AND CONFIDENCE

❖ The Lord is my Shepherd, I shall not want, there fore I have everything that I need

❖ The Joy of the LORD is my strength, therefore I can be and do all things through Christ Jesus who strengthens me

❖ GOD's goodness is following me His grace, mercy and favour is shadowing me daily

❖ I'm more than a conqueror, I am victorious and I win, because I acknowledge the Lord in all my ways

❖ Thank you Father for sensitive and attentive ears to hear what is needful and meaningful towards my well being

❖ I'm highly favored, blessed going in and I'm blessed coming out, it's all good, because I'm blessed like that

❖ I have favour with both GOD and man, because my ways pleases the LORD

❖ The windows of heaven are pouring out blessings to me, now, In the Name of Jesus

❖ Whatsoever my hands touch and do, shall prosper

❖ I'm doing my best, and it is good enough

- ❖ I do my best daily, therefore I have no reason to be jealous nor compete with others
- ❖ GOD has not given me the spirit of fear, but He has given and anointed me with power, love and a sound mind, therefore Dementia and Alzheimer's does not come near me
- ❖ Thank you, Father GOD, for relief, I thank you Lord for the peace
- ❖ Thank you Lord for removing the pricks and negative out of my atmosphere

AFFIRMATIONS
PROMOTION READY

- ❖ The Lord is my Shepherd, I shall not want
- ❖ I am blessed and highly favored
- ❖ Promotion cometh to me now, In The Name of Jesus
- ❖ I'm blessed with a new job and new assignments and I Thank you Jehovah Jireh, my provider
- ❖ Today, I have favour with both GOD and man, because my ways pleases the LORD
- ❖ The doors of opportunities are opened unto me, Thank you Lord for the open doors
- ❖ Whatsoever my hands touch, and my mind think shall prosper, because I'm like a tree planted by the rivers of water
- ❖ I have the tongue of the learned, therefore I know all things
- ❖ I thank you Lord for giving my tongue the pen of a ready writer
- ❖ I have ears to hear to what thus saith the LORD
- ❖ Thank you, Lord, for ordering my steps to a promotion, to an open door
- ❖ I'm blessed going in and I'm blessed coming out, I'm blessed, I'm blessed, I am blessed like that

AFFIRMATIONS
PROTECTION

- ❖ The Lord is my Shepherd, I shall not want
- ❖ If GOD is for me than who can be against me
- ❖ The LORD is on my side, therefore, I will not fear man
- ❖ GOD's goodness is following me His grace and mercy is shadowing me
- ❖ The Lord is my shield and buckler because I trust his every pure word
- ❖ The Lord is my shield and protector
- ❖ No weapon formed against me shall prosper
- ❖ Every tongue that rises against me in judgement, it shall be condemn
- ❖ The Lord has prepared me a table of goodness in the presence of my enemies
- ❖ Thank you, Lord, for always encamping your Angels around me and keeping me safe from all hurt, harm, danger and destruction, that is seen and unseen
- ❖ The Lord will fight might battles and enemies
- ❖ I thank you Lord that my goings and dwellings are safe and covered by you

AFFIRMATIONS
FAITHFULLY TRUSTING GOD

- ❖ My head, my mind is anointed with GOD's love and oil of joy
- ❖ I'm trying to be just, therefore my mind is blessed
- ❖ I have wisdom, revelation knowledge and understanding
- ❖ I am anointed, I am appointed to do GOD's will
- ❖ The Lord will order my steps with his word
- ❖ The word of GOD is a lamp unto my feet and a light for my paths
- ❖ I have the tongue of the learned, therefore I know all things
- ❖ The windows of heaven are pouring out blessings to me, to my family and neighbors
- ❖ I have ears to hear, therefore, I thank you Father GOD for the promotion with you and man
- ❖ The Lords goodness and mercy shall shadow and follow me daily
- ❖ I'm surrounded by the favour of GOD and there's a cloud of favour shadowing me now

AFFIRMATIONS
HEALTHY RELATIONSHIPS

* ❖ I have ears to hear to what thus saith the LORD
* ❖ The law of kindness is on my tongue at all times
* ❖ I will not do unto others as they have done unto me, unless it's something good
* ❖ I will pursue peace with all men
* ❖ I'm blessed, I'm a peacemaker, therefore I am a child of the Most High GOD
* ❖ I have favour with both GOD and man, because my ways please the LORD
* ❖ I thank you Father GOD that I owe no man nothing but respect and love, In the Name of Jesus
* ❖ I thank you Father GOD that like YOU, I have no respector of persons, but whomsoever will and whomsoever is in need
* ❖ Help me Father GOD to be patient, love others and not judge them
* ❖ I thank you Father GOD and please help me to forgive others seven times seventy, if they ask

AFFIRMATIONS
FINANCIAL

- ❖ The Lord is my Shepherd, I shall not want, therefore, I thank you Father GOD for supplying my every need and granting me the desires of my heart and allowing me to live in abundance
- ❖ Thank you, Lord, for teaching me how to profit and giving me the power to get wealth and empowering me to become and stay debt free
- ❖ I thank you Father GOD for giving me seeds to sow
- ❖ No good things will the Lord withhold from me because I'm trying my best to walk uprightly
- ❖ I thank you Father GOD for allowing me to give with a good measure, press down and shaken together to who you put on my mind and in my heart
- ❖ Thank you, Lord, for making me one of your servants and delighting in my prosperity
- ❖ I thank you Father GOD for the houses and land that I did not till, nor build, thank you Lord for the blessings of homes
- ❖ I thank you Father GOD that I owe no man nothing but respect and love, In the Name of Jesus

- ❖ The windows of heaven are pouring out financial blessings to me, right now. My financial accounts are overflowing with blessings and GOD's favor
- ❖ I thank you Father GOD for the wealth and riches that are in my home
- ❖ Thank you, Lord for houses that I didn't build and land that I didn't till, is paid in full
- ❖ Thank you, Father GOD for debt cancellation
- ❖ Thank you, Father GOD for debt free home, my mortgage is paid in full
- ❖ I thank you, Father GOD, that my vehicle is paid in full and my family's vehicles are too
- ❖ Thank you, Lord, for the debt cancellation
- ❖ Thank you, Father GOD, for allowing me to purchase all things with cash or same as cash transactions

CHAPTER **4** FOUR

WRONG WORDS

Blessings and curses come from the same heart, and mouth. Don't be negative and make the enemy happy by saying words of no value. Be positive, speak life, love and color into your presence and the lives of others. Tap into GOD's unlimited blessings.

It's not the materialistic things that cause emotions, strife and wrath to be stirred up, because they can't verbally talk; it is words, what was said that causes the negative discomfort in our atmosphere and space.

NEGATIVE VIBES

Saying affirmations, confessions and prayers on a regular basis, will cause us to have fewer negative encounters, situations, in our space and on our paths. We won't always be free of negative things, because if we were, then we wouldn't need GOD, or know about His goodness and loving kindness towards us; nor His methods that will deliver us and others from evil. Being *Born Again, (renewed mind with the **"word"** of GOD)* along with having an understanding about the enemy's thought process helps us to endure, push past the negative and dark tactics of the enemy (satan). It puts us in a cruise and drive mental awareness, while enjoying the lights of life and the brightness of GOD's kingdom.

THE WRONG WORDS

Saying or hearing the **wrong words** such as, I hate you, *can and may:*

- cause someone to run from love
- make a person despise someone else
- make someone want to hurt themselves and others
- cause a person to be poor, financially broke
- cause a curse to surface and linger
- allow someone to be defeated
- kill a relationship
- make someone feel terribly sad and bad
- cause someone to have thoughts of killing themselves or killing others
- cause conflict
- conclude people to think that they don't want to be in our presence, because of the harsh words that come forth out of our mouths.
- Negative words will leave us with regretful consequences. Even saying words such as *I love food* will probably cause someone to be overweight. There will be times when an echo or shadow may follow our words.

Words of silence have much value as well. Knowing when to speak and when to be quiet is knowledge to possess and cherish. *"I said, I will take heed to my ways, that I sin not with my tongue: <u>I will keep my mouth with a bridle, while the wicked is before me.</u> I was dumb with silence, I held my peace, even from good; and my sorrow was stirred. My heart was hot within me, while I was musing the fire burned: then spake I with my tongue, LORD, make me to know mine end, and the measure of my days, what it is; that I may know how frail I am".* Psalms 39:1-4

But, if we must say something, it's always beneficial to quietly mediate, and scope out the whole matter before we speak. Mediating on our words and thoughts will reward us with good outcomes regarding our situations and relationships. We don't want a life full of regrets, or "I wish I had of" after thoughts nor hind sights. We want to be solid and grounded, positioned to win.

The following are **W**ords *scripturally based* that justify how the <u>**wrong words**</u> will cause hurt, negative situations, and prohibit someone from having peace and positive things in their life. The scriptures also highlight negative words, their consequences, and repercussions.

Then Job answered and said, How long will ye vex my soul, and **break me in pieces with words**? These ten times have ye reproached me: ye are not ashamed that ye make yourselves strange to me.   Job 19:2

Come, ye children, hearken unto me: I will teach you the fear of the LORD. What man is he that desireth life, and loveth many days, that he may see good? **Keep thy tongue from evil, and thy lips from speaking guile**. Depart from evil, and do good; seek peace, and pursue it. The eyes of the LORD are upon the righteous, and his ears are open unto their cry.   Psalm 34:11-15

I said, I will take heed to my ways, **that I sin not with my tongue: I will keep my mouth with a bridle, while the wicked is before me**. **I was dumb with silence, I held my peace**, even from good; and my sorrow was stirred. My heart was hot within me, while I was musing the fire burned: **then spake I with my tongue**, LORD, make me to know mine end, and the measure of my days, what it is; that I may know how frail I am.   Psalms 39:1-4

(To the chief Musician, A Psalm of David.) Hold not thy peace, O GOD of my praise; **For the mouth of the wicked and the mouth of the deceitful are opened against me**:

they have spoken against me with a lying tongue. They compassed me about also **with words of hatred**; and fought against me without a cause. For my love they are my adversaries: but I give myself unto prayer. And they have rewarded me evil for good, and hatred for my love. Set thou a wicked man over him: and let satan stand at his right hand. When he shall be judged, let him be condemned: and let his prayer become sin.

Psalms 109-1-7

A naughty person, a wicked man, walketh with a froward mouth. He winketh with his eyes, he speaketh with his feet, he teacheth with his fingers; Frowardness *is* in his heart, he deviseth mischief continually; he soweth discord. Therefore shall his calamity come suddenly; suddenly shall he be broken without remedy.   Proverbs 6:12-15

The **mouth** of a righteous man **is a well of life**: but **violence covereth the mouth of the wicked**.

Proverbs 10:11

The **words of the wicked** *are* to lie in wait for blood: but **the mouth of the upright** shall deliver them.

Proverbs 12:6

The **wicked is snared by the transgression of _his_ lips**: but the just shall come out of trouble.   Proverbs 12:13

He that speaketh truth sheweth forth righteousness: but a false witness deceit. There is that **speaketh like the piercings of a sword**: but the tongue of the wise _is_ health. **The lip of truth shall be established for ever**: but a lying tongue _is_ but for a moment.   Proverbs 12:17-19

Lying lips are abomination to the LORD: but they that deal truly are his delight.   Proverbs 12:22

A **soft answer turneth away wrath**: but **grievous words stir up anger**. The **tongue of the wise** useth knowledge aright: but t**he mouth of fools poureth out foolishness**. The eyes of the LORD _are_ in every place, beholding the evil and the good. **A wholesome tongue _is_ a tree of life:** but perverseness therein _is_ a breach in the spirit.

Proverbs 15:1-4

The **lips of the wise disperse knowledge**: but the heart of the foolish _doeth_ not so.   Proverbs 15:7

The thoughts of the wicked _are_ an abomination to the LORD: **but the words of the pure are pleasant words**. He that is greedy of gain troubleth his own house; but he that hateth gifts shall live. The heart of the righteous studieth to answer: but **the mouth of the wicked poureth out evil things.** The LORD *is* far from the wicked: but he heareth the prayer of the righteous.   Proverbs 15:26-29

If thou hast done foolishly in lifting up thyself, or if thou hast thought evil, **lay thine hand upon though mouth**. Surely the churning of milk bringeth forth butter, and the wringing of the nose bringeth forth blood: **so the forcing of wrath bringeth forth strife**.   Proverbs 39:32

Wherefore I say unto you, All manner of sin and blasphemy shall be forgiven unto men: but the blasphemy against the Holy Ghost shall not be forgiven unto men. **And whosoever speaketh a word against the Son of man, it shall be forgiven him: but whosoever speaketh against the Holy Ghost, it shall not be forgiven him, neither in this world, neither in the world to come.** Either make the tree good, and his fruit good; or else make the tree corrupt, and his fruit corrupt: for the tree is known by his fruit. O generation of vipers, how can ye, being evil, speak good things? **for out of the abundance of the heart the mouth speaketh**. A good man out of the good treasure of the heart bringeth forth good things: and an evil man out of the evil treasure bringeth forth evil things. But I say unto you, That **every idle word** that men shall speak, they shall give account thereof in the day of judgment. **For by thy words thou shalt be justified, and by thy words thou shalt be condemned**.   Matthew 12:31-37

And he called the multitude, and said unto them, Hear, and understand: **Not that which goeth into the mouth defileth a man; but that which cometh out of the mouth, this defileth a man**. Then came his disciples, and said unto him, Knowest thou that the Pharisees were offended, after they heard this saying? But he answered and said, Every plant, which my heavenly Father hath not planted, shall be rooted up. Let them alone: they be blind leaders of the blind. And if the blind lead the blind, both shall fall into the ditch. Then answered Peter and said unto him, Declare unto us this parable. And Jesus said, Are ye also yet without understanding?

Do not ye yet understand, that whatsoever entereth in at the mouth goeth into the belly, and is cast out into the draught? But those things which proceed out of the mouth come forth from the heart; and they defile the man. For out of the heart proceed evil thoughts, murders, adulteries, fornications, thefts, false witness, blasphemies: These are *the things* which defile a man: but to eat with unwashen hands defileth not a man.   Matthew 15:10-20

My brethren, be not many masters, knowing that we shall receive the greater condemnation. For in many things we offend all. **If any man offend not in word, the same is a perfect man**, and able also to bridle the whole body. Behold, we put bits in the horses' mouths, that they may obey us; and we turn about their whole body. Behold also the ships, which though they be so great, and are driven of fierce winds, yet are they turned about with a very small helm, whithersoever the governor listeth. Even so **the tongue is a little member, and boasteth great things**. Behold, how great a matter a little fire kindleth! **And the tongue is a fire, a world of iniquity: so is the tongue among our members, that it defileth the whole body, and setteth on fire the course of nature; and it is set on fire of hell**. For every kind of beasts, and of birds, and of serpents, and of things in the sea, is tamed, and hath been tamed of mankind: **But the tongue can no man tame; it is an unruly evil, full of deadly poison.** Therewith bless we GOD, even the Father; and therewith curse we men, which are made after the similitude of GOD. **Out of the same mouth proceedeth blessing and cursing.** My brethren, these things ought not so to be.   James 3:1-10

Hold not thy peace, O GOD of my praise; For **the mouth of the wicked and the mouth of the deceitful are opened against me; they have spoken against me with a lying tongue.** They compassed me about also with words of hatred; and fought against me without a cause. For my love they are my adversaries: but I give myself unto prayer. And they have rewarded me evil for good and hatred for my love. Set thou a wicked man over him: and let satan stand at his right hand. When he shall be judged, let him be condemned; and let his prayer become sin. Let his days be few; and let another take his office. Psalm 109:1-8

CONFESSIONS, BIND AND LOOSE PRINCIPLES AND WARFARE:

(Armed conflict; war, fighting. any struggle or contest)

Confessions: An owning up; acknowledgment; admission; acknowledged of belief; profession of faith; belief acknowledged; creed; person who acknowledges belief (confessor)

PRAYERS FOR RELIEF AND WARFARE

BINDING AND LOOSING
Keys to the Kingdom of Heaven
Matthew 16:19

There is no direct and precise prayer in the bible regarding *binding and loosing*. But to *bind and loose* is the authoritative blessing that Jesus told Peter he would give him, because he *(Peter)* recognized who Jesus was. Jesus told Peter that he would give him keys to the kingdom of heaven and whatsoever he **loose on earth will be loosed in Heaven** and whatsoever **he bind on earth will be bound in Heaven.** *(Heaven is our backup for what we're hoping for)*

Keys give us permission to open doors and enter in. And a master key (keys from the MASTER of everything) will open all the doors in one facility (the World). Keys to the kingdom of heaven, *binding* and *loosing* will soundly change things for us with Heaven as our back-up; as well as our touch and agree partner.

Bind means that we're gathering *(saying something)* against all the negatives words, situations, attempts

63

and things that tries to kill, steal, destroy, prohibit, and stop us from fulfilling our purpose as well as goals. And *loose* means that we're bringing *(by saying something)* peace and the things we need into existence. We're getting rid of the negative forces in our lives and ushering in the positive. We're surrounding ourselves with moments of how things "ought to be" through the words we say and the actions we take.

Binding and *Loosing* can be utilized when we want something specifically to happen or not happen in our lives. I personally believe that it is a must strategy when situations are uneasy and dangerous. The *bind* and *loose* principles will bring you out of the danger zone, cause something to be eliminated. We will have an opportunity to experience a **"no more"** in our way, nor in our lives, that can sometimes come suddenly, when we utilize the bind and loose principles. "**When** *Jesus came into the coasts of Cesarea Philippi, he asked his disciples, saying, Whom do men say that I the Son of man am? And they said, Some say that thou art John the Baptist: some, Elias; and others, Jeremias, or one of the prophets. He saith unto them, But whom say ye that I am?*

And Simon Peter answered and said, Thou art the Christ, the Son of the living GOD. And Jesus answered and said unto him, **_Blessed art thou, Simon Barjona_**: for flesh and blood hath not revealed it unto thee, but my Father which is in heaven. And I say also unto thee, That thou art Peter, and upon this rock I will build my church; and the gates of hell shall not prevail against it. **_And I will give unto thee the keys of the kingdom of heaven: and whatsoever thou shalt bind on earth shall be bound in heaven: and whatsoever thou shalt loose on earth shall be loosed in heaven._** Then charged he his disciples that they should tell no man that he was Jesus the Christ".

Matthew 16:13-20

DAILY __PERSONAL__ LIFE CONFESSIONS

Through Decree and Establishment
(Critique to fit your needs)

FATHER GOD In the Name of Jesus, I think you that I can decree a thing and it shall be established, therefore:

- **I decree** and plead the Blood of Jesus, over my mind, body, soul and spirit, my comings, and goings. And I decree that no weapon formed against me shall prosper.

- **I decree** that I shall not die, but I shall live and declare the works of you LORD; __for I'm grateful and thankful__ that my times are in your hands, and your hands alone, O' LORD; therefore, **I decree** that "No weapon formed against me shall prosper and every tongue that rises against me in judgment, thou shall be condemn".
  And I thank you Father GOD, Jehavah Rohi, The Lord My Sheperd that everything pertaining to my life is in Devine order, **Through the Blood and In the Name of Jesus,** Amen.

Scriptures Regarding Life and Wellbeing

For then shalt thou have thou delight in the Almighty, and shalt lift up thy face unto GOD. Thou shalt make thy prayer unto him, and he shall hear thee, and thou shalt pay thy vows. Thou shalt also decree a thing, and it shall be established unto thee: and the light shall shine upon thy ways. Job 22:26-28

I shall not die, but live, and declare the works of the Lord.
Psalms 118:17

But I trusted in thee O Lord: I said, Thou art my GOD. My times are in thy hand: deliver me from the hand of mine enemies, and from them that persecute me.
Psalms 31:14-15

No weapon that is formed against thee shall prosper; and every tongue that shall rise against thee in judgment thou shall condemn. Isaiah 54:17

CONFESSIONS FOR YOUR
<u>PERSONAL</u> HEALTH

Through Bind and Loose Principles
(Critique to fit your needs and concerns)

I THANK YOU Father GOD, that <u>whatsoever I bind on Earth</u>, is <u>bound in Heaven</u>, and <u>whatsoever I loose on Earth is loosed in Heaven</u>, therefore,

I bind: anything and all things that tries to attack my mind, body, soul and spirit. I especially bind:

_____

Name it (them)

And **I loose:**

- that those infirmities, sicknesses until death, negative forces, the aches, diseases, germs, pain and viruses are no more, *In the Name of Jesus*, and **I loose** that they all have been *plucked up by the root and planted in the Sea*, and **Through the Blood and In the Name of Jesus,**

I loose that I am:

- Healed, Healthy and Whole; Blessed and Highly Favored. Free from all infirmities, healed from all sicknesses unto death, free of aches, diseases, germs, pain, and virus; for Jesus was wounded for my transgressions and bruised for my iniquities and the chastisement of my peace is upon You Father GOD, LORD Jesus and the Holy Spirit; And because of Jesus's stripes, love and sacrifice, I am healed. Thank you, Jehovah Rapha my Healer and Jehovah Rohi my Shepherd. I thank you Lord, **Through the Blood and In the Name of Jesus,** Amen.

Scriptures Regarding Healings

Jesus was wounded for our transgressions and bruised for our iniquities and the chastisement of our peace is upon him, and because of his strips, love and sacrifice, we are healed in every area of our lives.   Isaiah 53:5

Surely Lord, if you caused the man who was born blind, eventually see, surely you can heal my current health infirmity.   John 3:3

Surely Lord if you can heal someone who was possessed with a devil, blind and dumb, surely you can and will heal my infirmity or infirmities.   Matthew 12:22

SINGLE AND PRAYER TO HAVE A SPOUSE
Through Bind and Loose Principles

(Critique to fit your desires and needs) Warfare because two is better than one and the enemy doesn't like when GOD's Children become one in marriage. The enemy (serpent)also tried to bring division between Adam and Eve.

FATHER GOD in the Name of Jesus I thank you that whatsoever **I bind on Earth** is **bound** in Heaven and whatsoever **I loose on Earth** is **loosed** in Heaven, therefore *Through the Blood and In the Name of Jesus*

- **I bind** that I am no longer single and **I loose** my spouse
- **I bind** lust and sin out of my life and **I loose** holiness and righteousness I shall walk therein.
- **I bind** loneliness out of my life and **I loose** that your presence Father GOD is enough for me.
- **I bind** fake and phony Christians, suitors who try to seduce me into sin and **I loose** ears to hear and eyes to see in both the spiritual and natural. And I decree that I am not a silly woman, I am not a lustful man.

and **I decree** and **loose** that my spouse is a true warrior, child of you GOD. And that You Lord Jesus is first in their, (his or her) life.

- **I decree and loose** that my spouse is seeking you daily for instructions and directions.
- **I decree and loose** that my spouse will love righteousness and You, LORD with all their heart, mind, soul, and spirit.
- **I decree and loose** that my spouse have the gift of giving and saving.
- **I decree and loose** that my spouse will not be seduced by flattery words and sinful bodily suggestions.
- **I decree and loose** that my spouse will only have eyes and a desire for me.

And I pray that (**she** will respect me as Sarah respected Abraham, she called him lord) and that (**he** will love me as Christ loved the church.
I thank you Father GOD for my spouse, *In the Name of Jesus.*

Scriptures Regarding Marriage

Drink water out of thine own cistern, and running waters out of thine own well. Let thy fountains be dispersed abroad, and rivers of waters in the streets. Let them be only thine own and not strangers with thee. Let thy fountain be blessed: and rejoice with the wife of thy youth. Let her be as the loving hind and pleasant roe; let her breasts satisfy thee at all times; and be thou ravished always with her love.

Proverbs 5:15-19

Whoso findeth a wife, findeth a good thing, and obtaineth favour of the Lord.   Proverbs 18:22

Likewise, ye wives, be in subjection to your own husbands; that, if any obey not the word, they also may without the word be won by the conversation of the wives.

1 Peter 3:2-5

Your word says that two is better than one; because they have a good reward for their labour. For if they fall, the one will lift up his fellow: but woe to him that is alone when he falleth; for he hath not another to help him up.

Again, if two lie together, then they have heat: but how can one be warm alone? And if one prevails against him, two shall withstand him: and a threefold cord is not quickly broken. Ecclesiastes 4:9-12

FINANCIAL CONFESSION
Through Bind and Loose Principles
(Critique to fit your needs)

FATHER GOD in The Name of Jesus, You said that you delight in the prosperity of your servants. And that You will give me power to get wealth and teach me how to profit. *You said that You will supply my every need according to Your riches in glory through Christ Jesus,* Therefore, I thank you Father GOD, that whatsoever **I bind on Earth, is bound in Heaven**, and whatsoever **I loose on Earth is loosed in Heaven,** therefore, ***Through the Blood and In the Name of Jesus:***

I bind:

Name Your financial Concern(s)

_____

And I loose:

- that the **devour, hinderance, lack, debt and negative forces** that try to come against my finances, my purse, wallet, my relationships with financial institutions and financial blessings are no more and **I loose** that *they all have been plucked up by the root and planted in the Sea* and I thank you Lord, and **loose** that I, am prosperous, I'm wealthy, I have more than enough because of you Father GOD as El Shaddai, (more than enough) and Jehovah Jireth (my provider) and I thank you Father GOD, LORD Jesus and the Holy Spirit that I am blessed, highly favored and debt free, *Through the Blood and In the Name of Jesus. Amen.*

VARIOUS FINANCIAL CONCERNS TO BIND AND LOOSE (Pray)

• Student loan debt, (Put a name to the company)	• Business loan debt, (Put a name to it)
• Automobile debt, (Say the model and make)	• Home mortgage (rent) debt, (Say your address, city, state and zip code)
• Credit card debt, • Fruitless spending debt,	• The devour, hinderances and lack

Scriptures Regarding Finances

I thank you Father for giving me the power to get wealth.

Deuteronomy 8:18

I thank you for teaching me how to profit.   Isaiah 48:17

I thank you for not withholding no good things from me because I'm walking up rightly.   Psalms 84:11

I thank you Lord, for having pleasure in my prosperity, who is one of your servants.   Psalms 35:27

DAILY LIFE CONFESSIONS <u>CORPORATELY</u> OR FOR OTHERS
Through Decree and Establishment
(Critique to fit your needs)

FATHER GOD *In the Name of Jesus*, I think you that I can decree a thing and it shall be established, therefore:

I decree and plead the Blood of Jesus, over my mind, body, soul and spirit, my comings, and goings. And I decree that no weapon formed against me shall prosper.

I decree that:

_____
Your choice of name(s)

shall not die but (he, she, they) shall live and declare the works of you LORD; **and I pray** that their

_____
Use either of the following: (his, her, their, them)

times are in your hands, O' LORD and your hands alone, therefore **I decree** that No weapon formed against (him, her, them) shall prosper. *And I thank you LORD,* ***Through the Blood and In the Name of Jesus,*** *Amen.*

Scriptures Regarding Life and Wellbeing

For then shalt thou have thou delight in the Almighty, and shalt lift up thy face unto GOD. Thou shalt make thy prayer unto him, and he shall hear thee, and thou shalt pay thy vows. Thou shalt also decree a thing, and it shall be established unto thee: and the light shall shine upon thy ways.   Job 22:26-28

I shall not die, but live, and declare the works of the Lord.
Psalms 118:17

But I trusted in thee O Lord: I said, Thou art my GOD. My times are in thy hand: deliver me from the hand of mine enemies, and from them that persecute me.
Psalms 31:14-15

No weapon that is formed against thee shall prosper; and every tongue that shall rise against thee in judgment thou shall condemn.   Isaiah 54:17

HEALED AND HEALTHY
Through Bind and Loose Principles
(Critique to fit your needs and concerns)

I THANK YOU Father GOD, that whatsoever I bind on Earth, is bound in Heaven, and whatsoever I loose on Earth is loosed in Heaven. Your **"word"** says that Jesus was wounded for our transgressions and bruised for our iniquities and that the chastisement of our peace is upon him, therefore, ***Through the Blood and In the Name of Jesus, I bind:***

Name it (them)

That comes to attack my (his, her, their, our) mind, body, soul and spirit.

I loose:
- that those infirmities, negative forces, are no more, **In the Name of Jesus**, *they have all been plucked up by the root and planted in the Sea*, Through **The Blood and In the Name of Jesus,**

I loose: that I am
- Healed, Healthy and Whole; Blessed and Highly Favored. Free from all infirmities, healed from all sicknesses unto death, free of aches, diseases,

germs, pain, and virus; For you, Jesus was wounded for (my) our transgressions and bruised for (my) our iniquities and the chastisement of (my) our peace is upon you Jesus and because of your stripes, love and sacrifice, (we, I am, they are) healed. Thank you Jehovah Rapha our Healer and Jehovah Rohi our Shepherd. I thank you, **Through the Blood and In the Name of Jesus**, *Amen*.

VARIOUS HEALTH ISSUES TO
BIND AND LOOSE (PRAY)

• Coronavirus *(Covid-19)* • Delta variant virus • Mu variant virus • Omicron virus • Flurona • Omicron - Ba2, Ba4 and Ba5 viruses • Covid Variant EG.5 (Eris)	• Respiratory issues – *(diseases, germs, and viruses)* • HIV Aids positive results • HIV Aids *(diseases, germs and viruses)* • Ebola virus • Monkey-pox virus • Bacteria and Fungus – *(diseases, germs, and viruses)*
• (ALL) Aches, Disease, Germs, Pain, and Viruses • Arthritis & Inflammation • Blood Clots • Baker Cyst • Leukemia traits and cells • Cancer traits and cells	• Aneurysms • Heart attacks • Strokes • Stress • Diabetes • High Blood Pressure (Hypertension)
All sicknesses unto death Every ache, disease, germ, all pain and viruses	
that tries to attack my mind, body, soul and spirit	

VARIOUS HEALTH ISSUES
TO BIND AND LOOSE (PRAY)

• Bladder failure • Heart failure • Kidney failure • Liver failure • Lung failure	• Vernal diseases • Pink eye • Canker sores
• Autism • Down syndrome • Cerebral palsy • Crib death SIDS – (sudden infant death syndrome) • Polio	• Alzheimer's • Dementia • Multiple Sclerosis • Cataracts • Glaucoma • Hearing loss • Shingles
• Breast cancer • Ovarian cancer • Prostate cancer • Female issues; Hysterectomies and Uterus • Male & Female negative reproductive issues	• Emotional, mental and physical illness • Emotional, mental and physical oppression • Homosexuality • Low self-esteem • Bullying • Suicide
All sicknesses unto death Every ache, disease, germ, all pain and viruses	
that tries to attack my mind, body, soul and spirit	

Scriptures Regarding Healings

Jesus was wounded for our transgressions and bruised for our iniquities and the chastisement of our peace is upon him, and because of his strips, love and sacrifice, we are healed in every area of our lives.   Isaiah 53:5

Surely Lord, if you caused the man who was born blind, eventually see, surely you can heal my current health infirmity.   John 3:3

Surely Lord if you can heal someone who was possessed with a devil, blind and dumb, surely you can and will heal my infirmity or infirmities.   Matthew 12:22

REGARDING <u>RELATIONSHIPS</u> CORPORATELY
Through Bind and Loose Principles
(Critique to fit your concerns)

FATHER GOD *In the Name of Jesus,* "Your **"word"** says, *How good and pleasant it is for brethren (man) to dwell together in unity"* Psalms 133:1. Your word also says, *to do unto others as we would have them to do unto us,* and that *people will know we are Your disciples by the way we love one another;* So, therefore, I bring before you relationships between:

Your choice

or

*See various and suggested relationships
<hr>

I (we) bind:

- the anger, animosity, bitterness, bondage, unhealthy control, competitiveness, discord, deceit, division, envy, evil, unforgiveness, friction, friendly fire, hatred, iniquity, jealous, malice, manipulation, misunderstanding, murder, rebellious, rebellion, sin, strife, wickedness, and wrath, that tries to:

destroy, harm, hinder, hurt, interfere, provoke and prohibit healthy relationships; **I loose** that they are no more *Through the Blood and In the Name of Jesus.*

I (we) loose:
- that those negative spirits, actions, forces, evil thinking, thoughts, words, characteristics, and personalities, are no more. They *all have been plucked up by the root and planted in the Sea*, and *Through the Blood and In the Name of Jesus,*

I (we) loose:
- that those relationships are now: healed, healthy and whole, they have joy, love and peace, there is forgiveness, respect, an understanding, and unity.

I (we) continue to loose and thank you
- Father GOD, Lord Jesus and The Holy Spirit for standing at the gates and doors of those relationships.

I (we) continue to loose and thank you Father GOD *In the Name of Jesus* for Changing, Helping, Refreshing, Renewing and Restoring those relationships, especially those You Lord have predestined and ordained. I touch and agree that who You have joined together Lord, let no man put asunder, **_Through the Blood and In the Name of Jesus,_** _Amen._

*VARIOUS AND SUGGESTED RELATIONSHIPS

FATHER GOD in the Name of Jesus, **<u>I bring before you</u>** relationships between:
- You and man, whom You created in YOUR image.
- You and woman whom You strategically created with purpose.
- Families: grandparents, aunts and uncles, nieces and nephews, and cousins.

<u>I bring before you</u> relationships between:
- adopted families, blended families, extended families, foster families, in-laws, and stepfamilies.

<u>I bring before you Father GOD</u> relationships between:
- those who live in the
- same home,
- apartment,
- on the same street, on the same block.

<u>I bring before You</u> relationships between:
- friends, The Body of Christ, neighbors, associates,
- cities, townships, counties, states, and countries throughout the World.

I bring before you relationships between:

- universities and college roommates,
- universities and college students on university and colleges premises,
- relationships between universities and college students and the faculty, Presidents, Vice Presidents, Dean, Professors, Counselors, Financial Advisors and those who are employed, and volunteer at Universities and Colleges.

I bring before you relationships between:

- students in the classroom,
- students on school premises,
- relationships between students and teachers, administrators and those who are employed and who volunteer with school districts, from pre-school – high school and all sectors of education.

I bring before you Father GOD relationships between:

- juvenile delinquent children in juvenile delinquent facilities,
- relationships between juvenile delinquent children and the employees and workers in juvenile delinquent facilities.

I bring before you Father GOD relationships between:

- men and women who are incarcerated, in prisons and jails.

I bring before you relationships between:

- men and women who are incarcerated in prisons and jails and the employees, volunteers and workers.

Father GOD, I bring before you relationships between:

- pedestrians, bicycle riders, automobile drivers, motorcycle riders, truck drivers and those who chauffer, (drive) and ride public transportation.

I bring before you Father GOD relationships between:

- co-workers, relationships between employer and employees.

I bring before you relationships between:

- entrepreneurs, business owners, and their clients, creditors and customers.

I bring before you relationships between:

- those who own sporting teams and arenas, their employees, and those who attend athletic events, at sporting arena venues, in schools, in the neighborhood, recreation centers, neighborhood parks and even during the Olympics.

I bring before you relationships between:

- athletic teams, athletes and the owner of athletic teams, captains, coaches, leaders, managers and officials during sporting events.

I bring before you relationships between:

- athletes and their fans, those who are personally employed by them, and those who help, assist and support them.

I bring before you relationships between:

- various branches of the Military (Armed Forces); the Air Force, Army, Coast Guard, Marines, National Guard, Navy and Navy Seals.

I bring before you Father GOD, relationships between:

- First Responders, Law Enforcement, among themselves and between those who they service, protect and defend and citizens.

I bring before you Father GOD relationships between:

- politicians, politicians and their constituents, appointed and elected officials and political parties.

I bring before you Father GOD relationships between:

- (World Leaders) Presidents, Vice Presidents, US Speaker of the House, US Secretary of State, US Secretary of Defense, US Chief of Staff, Prime Ministers, Premiers, Kings, Queens, those who are a Princes, a Princess, Chancellors, Ambassadors, Embassies, Religious Leaders: The Five-fold Ministry, Priest, the Pope and Missionaries throughout the World.

Scriptures Regarding Relationships

How good and pleasant it is when men dwell together in unity.   Psalms 133:1

People will know that we are Jesus's disciples by the love we show one another.   John 13:35

*Lord your "**word**" says that we shall forgive seven times in a day, help us Lord to forgive those who have repented from the trespass and hurt they did unto us.   Luke 17:4*

And as ye would that men should do to you, do ye also to them likewise.   Luke 6:31

*Your "**word**" also says to let us consider one another, to provoke unto love and to good works. Not forsake the assembling of ourselves together, as the manner of some is; but exhorting one another.   Hebrews 10:24-25*

CHAPTER **6** SIX

BIBLICAL PRAYERS

DON'T PRAY TO BE SEEN
Matthew 6:4-8

How Jesus Says we *should not* pray.

And when thou prayest, thou shalt not be as the hypocrites are: for they love to pray standing in the synagogues and in the corners of the streets, that they may be seen of men. Verily I say unto you, They have their reward. But thou, when thou prayest, enter into thy closet, and when thou hast shut thy door, pray to thy Father which is in secret; and thy Father which seeth in secret shall reward thee openly. **But when ye pray**, use not vain repetitions, as the heathen do: for they think that they shall be heard for their much speaking. Be not ye therefore like unto them: for your Father knoweth what things ye have need of, before ye ask him.

THE MODEL PRAYER
Luke 11:1-4

How Jesus Says we *should* pray.

And it came to pass, that, as he was praying in a certain place, when he ceased, one of his disciples said unto him, **Lord, teach us to pray**, as John also taught his disciples. And he said unto them, **When ye pray, say**, Our Father which art in heaven, Hallowed be thy name. Thy kingdom come. Thy will be done, as in heaven, so in earth. Give us day by day our daily bread. And forgive us our sins; for we also forgive every one that is indebted to us. And lead us not into temptation; but deliver us from evil.

JESUS PRAYS
John 17:9

"I pray for them: I pray not for the world, but for them which thou hast given me; for they are thine."

CONFESSIONAL PRAYER

Psalms 23

A powerful personal prayer to say about yourself daily for
strength, hope and guidance.
It's loaded with benefits and a covering.

The Lord is my shepherd; I shall not want. He
maketh me to lie down in green pastures: he leadeth
me beside the still waters. He restoreth my soul: he
leadeth me beside the still waters. He restoreth my
soul: he leadeth me in the paths of righteousness for
his name's sake. Yea, though I walk through the valley
of the shadow of death, I will fear no evil: for thou art
with me; thy rod and thy staff they comfort me. Thou
preparest a table before me in the presence of mine
enemies: thou anointest my head with oil, my cup
runneth over. Surely goodness and mercy shall follow
me all the days of my life: and I will dwell in the house
of the Lord for ever.

CONFESSIONAL PRAYER
Psalms 121

A prayer that uplifts, gives peace, comfort and
makes you feel safe.

I will lift up mine eyes unto the hills, from whence
cometh my help. My help cometh from the Lord,
which made heaven and earth. He will not suffer thy
foot to be moved: he that keepeth thee will not
slumber: Behold, he that keepeth Israel shall neither
slumber nor sleep. The LORD is thy keeper: the
LORD is thy shade upon thy right hand. The sun
shall not smite thee by day, nor the moon by night.
The LORD shall preserve thee from all evil: he shall
preserve thy going out and thy coming in from this
time forth, and even for evermore.

Submitted by: *Destini's J. Stephens*

PRAYER OF SUPPPLICATION FOR TROUBLE TO CEASE
Psalms 142:1-7

When you think no one cares or understands.

I cried unto the LORD with my voice; with my voice unto the LORD did I make my supplication. I poured out my complaint before Him; I shewed before him my trouble. When my spirit was overwhelmed within me, then thou knewest my path. In the way wherein I walked have they privily laid a snare for me. I looked on my right hand, and beheld, but there was no man that would know me: refuge failed me; no man care for my soul.

I cried unto thee, O LORD: I said, Thou art my refuge and my portion in the land of the living. Attend unto my cry; for I am brought very low: deliver me from my persecutors; for they are stronger than I. Bring my soul out of prison, that I may praise thy name: the righteous shall compass me about; for thou shalt deal bountifully with me.

PRAYER OF SUPPLICATION
RELIEF FROM ENEMIES
Psalms 143:1-9

Prayer for grace and mercy, after trusting
and following the enemy.

Hear my prayer, O LORD, give ear to my
supplication: in thy faithfulness answer me, and in
thy righteousness. And enter not judgment with thy
servant: for in thy sight shall no man living be
justified. For the enemy hath persecuted my soul; he
hath smitten my life down to the ground; he hath
made me to dwell in darkness, as those that have
been dead. Therefore is my spirit overwhelmed with
me; my heart within me is desolate. I remember the
days of old; I meditate on all thy works; I muse on the
work of thy hands. I stretch forth my hands unto
thee: my soul thirsteth after thee, as a thirsty land.
Selah. *(a word of unknown meaning occurring frequently in the
Psalms, perhaps a musical direction indicating pause)*
Hear me speedily, O LORD; my spirit faileth: hide not
they face from me, lest I be like unto them that go

down into the pit. Cause me to hear thy lovingkindness in the morning; for in thee do I trust: cause me to know the way wherein I should walk; for I lift up my soul unto thee.

TOTALLY AND ONLY TRUSTING GOD
Jeremiah 17:5-8

Thus saith the LORD; *Cursed be the man that trusteth in man, and maketh flesh his arm, and whose heart departeth from the LORD.* For he shall be like the heath in the desert, and shall not see when good cometh; but shall inhabit the parched places in the wilderness, in a salt land and not inhabited. *Blessed is the man that trusteth in the LORD,* and *whose hope the LORD is.* For he shall be as a tree planted by the waters, and that spreadeth out her roots by the river, and shall not see when heat cometh, but her leaf shall be green; and shall not be careful in the year of drought, neither shall cease from yielding fruit. *Submitted by Tony L. Mills, Sr.*

ASK, SEEK AND KNOCK
Luke 11:5-10

Directives from Jesus, asking and letting the Lord know what you need; believing that you will have what you have asked him for.

And he said unto them, Which of you shall have a friend, and shall go unto him at midnight, and say unto him, Friend, lend me three loaves; For a friend of mine in his journey is come to me, and I have nothing to set before him? And he from within shall answer and say, Trouble me not: the door is now shut, and my children are with me in bed; I cannot rise and give thee. I say unto you, Though he will not rise and give him, because he is his friend, yet because of his importunity he will rise and give him as many as he needeth. And I say unto you, **Ask,** and it shall be given you; seek, and ye shall find; knock, and it shall be opened unto you. For **every one that asketh receiveth**; and he that seeketh findeth; and to him that knocketh it shall be opened.

PRAYER FOR ALL
1 Timothy 2:1-6

I exhort therefore that, first of all, **supplications, prayers, intercessions, and giving of thanks**, be made for all men; For kings, and for all that are in authority that we may lead a quiet and peaceable life in all godliness and honesty. For this is good and acceptable in the sight of GOD our Saviour; Who will have all men to be saved, and to come unto the knowledge of the truth. For there is one GOD, and one mediator between GOD and men, the man Christ Jesus; Who gave himself a ransom for all, to be testified in due time.

ONCE BLIND, BUT CAN NOW SEE
Matthew 9:27-31

And when Jesus departed thence, two blind men followed him, **crying, and saying**, Thou Son of David, have mercy on us. And when he was come into the house, the blind men came to him: and **Jesus saith unto them**, Believe ye that I am able to do this? They **said unto him, Yea, Lord. Then touched he their eyes, saying, According to your faith be it unto you**. And their eyes were opened; and Jesus straitly charged them, saying, See that no man know it. But they, when they were departed, spread abroad his fame in all that country.

FAITH, KNOWING WHAT TO SAY
Matthew 15:21-28

Then Jesus went thence, and departed into the coasts of Tyre and Sidon. And, behold, a woman of Canaan came out of the same coasts, and cried unto him, saying, Have mercy on me, O Lord, *thou* Son of David; my daughter is grievously vexed with a devil. But he answered her not a word. And his disciples came and besought him, saying, Send her away; for she crieth after us. But he answered and said, I am not sent but unto the lost sheep of the house of Israel. **Then came she and worshipped him, saying, Lord, help me**. But he answered and said, It is not meet to take the children's bread, and to cast it to dogs. **And she said, Truth, Lord: yet the dogs eat of the crumbs which fall from their masters' table.** Then Jesus answered and said unto her, O woman, **great is thy faith**: be it unto thee even as thou wilt. And her daughter was made whole from that very hour.

TRUSTING GOD AND KNOWING JESUS
Luke 7:1-10

Now when he had ended all his sayings in the audience of the people, he entered into Capernaum. And a certain centurion's servant, who was dear unto him, was sick, and ready to die. And when he heard of Jesus, he sent unto him the elders of the Jews, beseeching him that he would come and heal his servant. And when they came to Jesus, they besought him instantly, saying, That he was worthy for whom he should do this: For he loveth our nation, and he hath built us a synagogue. Then Jesus went with them. And when he was now not far from the house, the centurion sent friends to him, saying unto him, Lord, trouble not thyself: for I am not worthy that thou shouldest enter under my roof: Wherefore neither thought I myself worthy to come unto thee: **but say in a word, and my servant shall be healed**. For I also am a man set under authority, having under me soldiers, and I say unto one, Go, and he goeth; and to another, Come, and he cometh; and to my servant, Do this, and he doeth it.

When Jesus heard these things, he marvelled at him, and turned him about, and said unto the people that followed him, I say unto you, I have not found so great faith, no not in Israel. And they that were sent, returning to the house, found the servant whole that had been sick.

PRAYER OF RELIEF AND PROTECTION
Psalms 64:1-10

Hear my voice, O GOD, in my prayer: preserve my life from fear of the enemy. Hide me from the secret counsel of the wicked; from the insurrection of the workers of iniquity: **Who whet their tongue like a sword, and bend their bows to shoot their arrows, even bitter words**: That they may shoot in secret at the perfect: suddenly do they shoot at him, and fear not. They encourage themselves in an evil matter: they commune of laying snares privily; they say, Who shall see them? They search out iniquities; they accomplish a diligent search: both the inward thought of every one of them, and the heart, is deep. But GOD shall shoot at them with an arrow; suddenly shall they be wounded. **So they shall make their own tongue to fall upon themselves**: all that see them shall flee away. And all men shall fear, and shall declare the work of GOD; for they shall wisely consider of his doing. The righteous shall be glad in the LORD, and shall trust in him; and all the upright in heart shall glory.

DESPERATE PRAYER FROM THE HEART
Psalms 66:16-20

Come and hear, all ye that fear GOD, and I will declare what he hath done for my soul. **I cried unto him with my mouth, and he was extolled with my tongue**. If I regard iniquity in my heart, the Lord will not hear me: But Blessed be GOD, which hath not turned away my prayer, nor his mercy from me.

SAYING WHAT IS MEANINGFUL AND
FULL OF LIFE
Luke 12:1-5

In the mean time, when there were gathered together an innumerable multitude of people, insomuch that they trod one upon another, he began to say unto his disciples first of all, Beware ye of the leaven (actions) of the Pharisees, which is hypocrisy. For there is nothing covered, that shall not be revealed; neither hid, that shall not be known. Therefore **whatsoever ye have spoken in darkness shall be heard in the light; and that which ye have spoken in the ear in closets shall be proclaimed up on housetops**, And I say unto you my friends, Be not afraid of them that kill the body, and after that have no more that they can do. But I will forewarn you whom you shall fear: Fear him, which after he hath killed hath power to cast into hell; yea, I say unto you, Fear him.

PRAYER OF HEALING
Psalms 107:20

I thank you Father GOD for sending a word to heal and help me. I thank you Father for delivering me from all things destructive. I thank you Father GOD for your healing touch, mercies and grace.

PRAYER for HEALING
Jeremiah 17:14

Heal me, O Lord, and I shall be healed; save me and I shall be saved: for thou art my praise.

PRAYING for WHAT YOU NEED and WANT
Ruth 2:7

And she said, **I pray you, let me glean and gather after the reapers** among the sheaves: so she came, and hath continued even from the morning until now, that she tarried a little in the house.

A PRAYER OF WORSHIP
Psalms 141:2

Let my prayer be set forth before thee as incense; and the lifting up of my hands as the evening sacrifice.

A PRAYER of SUPPLICATION
Jeremiah 37:20

Therefore, hear now, I pray thee, O my Lord the king: let my supplication, I pray thee, be accepted before thee; that thou cause me not to return to the house of Jonathan the scribe, lest I die there.

HOW JESUS PRAYED as
INSTRUCTED by FATHER GOD
John 17:9

I pray for them: I pray not for the world, but for them which thou hast given me; for they are thine.

PRAYER FOR SAFETY AND SPIRITUAL STRENGTH BECAUSE OF THE ATTACKS FROM ENEMEIES

Psalms 55:16-22

As for me, I will call upon GOD; and the LORD shall save me. Evening, and morning, and at noon, will I pray, and cry aloud: and he shall hear my voice. He hath delivered my soul in peace from the battle that was against me: for there were many with me. GOD shall hear, and afflict them, even he that abideth of old. Selah. Because they have no changes, therefore thy fear not GOD. He hath put forth his hands against such as be at peace with him: he hath broken his covenant. The words of his mouth were smoother than butter, but war was in his heart: his words were softer than oil, yet were they drawn swords. Cast thy burden upon the LORD, and he shall sustain thee: he shall never suffer the righteous to be moved.

WELCOME PRAYER
Philippians 1:1-11

A pleasant greeting and words of truth and
encouragement about Jesus, that
Paul would take to those he was sent to.

Paul and Timotheus, the servants of Jesus Christ,
to all the saints in Christ Jesus which are at Philippi,
with the bishops and deacons: Grace *be* unto you, and
peace, from GOD our Father, and from the Lord Jesus
Christ. I thank my GOD upon every remembrance of
you, Always in every prayer of mine for you all
making request with joy, For your fellowship in the
gospel from the first day until now; Being confident
of this very thing, that he which hath begun a good
work in you will perform it until the day of Jesus
Christ: Even as it is meet for me to think this of you
all, because I have you in my heart; inasmuch as both
in my bonds, and in the defence and confirmation of
the gospel, ye all are partakers of my grace. For GOD
is my record, how greatly I long after you all in the
bowels of Jesus Christ. And this I pray, that your love

may abound yet more and more in knowledge
and in all judgment; That ye may approve things that
are excellent; that ye may be sincere and without
offence till the day of Christ; Being filled with the
fruits of righteousness, which are by Jesus Christ,
unto the glory and praise of GOD.

BENEDICTION PRAYER
Philippians 4:4-23

A prayer for the well being of those who
attended the gathering.

Rejoice in the Lord alway: and again I say,
Rejoice. Let your moderation be known unto all men.
The Lord is at hand. Be careful for nothing; but in
every thing by prayer and supplication with
thanksgiving let your requests be made known unto
GOD. And the peace of GOD, which passeth all
understanding, shall keep your hearts and minds
through Christ Jesus. **Finally, brethren**, whatsoever
things are true, whatsoever things are honest,

whatsoever things are just, whatsoever things are pure, whatsoever things are lovely, whatsoever things are of good report; if there be any virtue, and if there be any praise, think on these things. **Those things, which ye have both learned, and received, and heard, and seen in me, do: and the GOD of peace shall be with you**.

But my GOD shall supply all your need according to his riches in glory by Christ Jesus.   Philippians 4:4-9

Now unto GOD and our Father be glory for ever and ever. Amen. Salute every saint in Christ Jesus. The brethren which are with me greet you. All the saints salute you, chiefly they that are of Caesar's household. The grace of our Lord Jesus Christ be with you all. Amen.

Philippians 4:19-23

CHAPTER **7** SEVEN

HEARTFELT PRAYERS

PRAYER OF ADORATION

A Personable and Intimate Prayer
to Father GOD

FATHER GOD *In the Name of Jesus, Your only Begotten Son,* I thank you Father GOD for being You. I thank you loving for me unconditionally. I thank you for calling me out of darkness and into your marvelous light.

You Father GOD are worthy to be praise for all things and all matters. Thank you for leading me and guiding me. Thank you for protecting me. Thank you for keeping me in my right mind. Thank you for going before me and making every crooked path straight. Thank you for opening doors that no man can shut, and closing doors that no man can open.

You are Omnipotent, you're greater than great. You are the Wonderful Counselor, Mighty GOD, my everlasting Father, the Prince of Peace, King of Kings, Lord of Lords, my High Tower, a place of safety. You are my strength, the love of my life. I am lost without you. I'm grateful to be in your presence and honored to call you FATHER. I love you Lord and I'm so grateful for You, *In Jesus Name, Amen.*

A PERSONAL PRAYER OF THANKS
<u>AND ADORATION TO FATHER GOD</u>

FATHER GOD In the Name of Jesus I thank you for today. I thank you for strength, peace and love. I thank you for watching over me all night long, and not just me, but my family, friends, the body of Christ and neighbors. You are a good GOD an everlasting GOD, my friend, my high tower, my peace and my hope. Thank you for loving me unconditionally, thanks for guiding and helping me. Thank you, Father GOD, *In the Name of Jesus.*

<u>HUMBLED PRAYER OF THANKS</u>

You are my high tower the love of my life. I love you because you first love me. You have watched over me, guided me, helped and protected me. And I am very grateful. Help me to love like you love, unconditionally, help, help me; help me to stay humble and forever rooted in you, *Amen and In the Name of Jesus I pray.*

GRATEFUL PRAYER

I love You Lord, because You first loved me. You have called me out of darkness into your wonderful and marvelous light. You have ordered my steps with your word. You have kept me from all hurt, harm and danger, seen and unseen. You have reminded me to be quite and stay focused. Thank you, Father GOD, *In the Name of Jesus.*

PRAYER FOR SPOUSE

I thank you Father GOD that my Spouse is someone after your own heart. I pray that no one sits on the throne of my spouse's life but you LORD. I pray that my spouse thirst and desire holiness and righteousness. I pray that my spouse is a person of integrity and that their personal affairs, children,

116

household and finances are in a decent and ordered state. I pray that my spouse daily seeks you for inspiration, instructions and direction. Help me LORD to be forgiving with understanding towards my spouse. Help me LORD to live my life in such a way that I will draw my spouse and others to you LORD and you alone. These things I pray *In the Majestic Name of Your Son Jesus, Amen and Amen.*

PRAYER FOR HUSBAND

I thank you Father GOD that my husband is a man after your heart Father GOD. And that he fears the Lord and shuns every evil way. I thank you that he thirst, pants for holiness and righteousness, and that mercy and truth is in his heart. I thank you that he trust in you Lord with all his heart. I thank you that he has sound wisdom, discretion and understanding.

Thank you that he is both attractive inwardly and outwardly. I thank you that he is not slothful and what's so ever his hands do and touch, they shall prosper. I thank you that my husband is prosperous, and that he gives with purpose. I pray that he doesn't leave the paths of uprightness, to walk in darkness. I pray that my husband will not be flattered with words of a strange and stray woman. And that he doesn't lust after her beauty, but he adores and embraces me, his wife. I pray that he's not barren, his quiver is filled and full with the number of children he desires. And he loves you, Lord GOD with all his might. I thank and appreciate you LORD for my husband. *Through the Blood and In the Name of Jesus I pray, Amen.*

PRAYER FOR WIFE

I thank you Father GOD for giving me favor with you and my wife. I thank you that she is not a silly woman. I thank you that she builds and beautify our home with loving kindness. I thank you that she is a virtuous woman and that she doesn't bring shame to me, our children nor family. I thank you that I can trust her. I thank you that she desires to do me good and not evil daily. I thank you, that she delights in my warm touches and embracement.

I thank you that the law of kindness is on her tongue to whoever she encounters. I thank you that she's pleasing to my eyes and that her beauty inward and outwardly is better than, rubies and roses, emeralds and evening sunsets and diamonds and daises.

Thank you Lord for my wife. Teach, help and show me how to be satisfied in You, Oh Lord and appreciate my wife. *In the Name of Jesus, Amen.*

PRAYER FOR CHILDREN

I thank you Father GOD for (my, our) children. And I plead the Blood of Jesus over their mind, body, soul and spirit. And I decree, that no weapon formed against them shall prosper, and every tongue that rises against them in judgement, shall be condemn. I pray that you will keep the safe from all hurt, harm and danger, seen and unseen. I thank you that they are obedient. I pray that they won't forget your commandments Father GOD. I pray they will listen to the Godly instructions of (us, their parents, mother or father or guardian and grandparents as well). I thank you that my daughter is not silly, but a wise and virtuous daughter; and that she doesn't depart from the teachings of her youth.

I thank you that my son is not an evil man who speaketh froward things nor uses profanity. I thank you that my son take fast hold of instructions, especially your instructions Father GOD. I pray that he will not be captured by the lust of a silly, strange, flattery word girl, woman. I pray that my children will not be enticed by sinners but fear the Lord and depart from all evil. I pray that you Lord will daily order their steps with your wisdom.

I pray that you LORD will guard their ear and eye gates. And may they honor (me, their mother, me their father or those who have authority over them); and may they always take heed to the instructions and laws of us both.

Thank you, LORD, for my children and help (me, the parent, guardian) to carry, conduct myself in a way that they would be proud to call me, their mom, blessed and call their dad, honorable. Give me Father GOD the wisdom of a parent and help me to be caring, a blessing and not an enabler, nor hinderance to my children. Help me to teach and show them how to be honest, responsible, productive and caring individuals. I **bind** sin in their lives, and I **loose** Holiness and righteousness they shall walk their in. *Through the Blood and In the Name of Jesus, Amen.*

FROM THE HEART OF
MAN OF GOD, FATHER, HUSBAND,
SON AND BROTHER
By: LARRY J. JOHNSON, I

Dear Lord, I'm coming in prayer thanking you for waking me up this morning. This is the day you have made I will rejoice and be glad in it, (Psalms 118:24). Thank you for being a shield, and protection for me and my family, thank you so much because we need you. And Lord I know it's people all around the world that might need a special prayer as we speak, I pray that you comfort them, Lord. And I thank you for the joy and peace that you give me Lord, for keeping my mind on you and trusting you, it is the best feeling!!! (Isaiah 26:3). *In Your Name I Pray Jesus, Amen. Larry J. Johnson, I*

PRAYER FOR FAMILIES

We thank you Father GOD for our family. I thank you that we are a family on one accord. We thank you Father GOD that your word says that's it's good for brethren to dwell together in unity. Therefore, We thank you for the unity that's in our family. We thank you for teaching us how to help one another and not hinder each other. We thank you that what's theirs is mines and with is mine is theirs. We thank you that we love to share. We thank you that the law of kindness is on our tongues towards one another. We thank you that we are one Father GOD as you, Lord Jesus and the Holy Spirit are one. We thank you that we don't judge one another, only help. We thank you for reminding us to encourage one another daily. And we thank you Father GOD that we don't compete with one another only compliment each other. We thank you Father GOD for our precious, prosperous and loving Family. *In the Name of Jesus, we Pray.*

FROM THE HEART OF
A MOTHER, WOMAN OF GOD, DAUGHTER, SISTER AND FRIEND
By: CRYSTAL STEPHENS

Dear Father, We declare that this is the day you have made, we will rejoice and be glad in it. Save now Oh Lord, Oh Lord we beseech thee that you send now prosperity. We call it in from the north, south, east and west. We thank you that peace is in our home and prosperity in our palaces. And because of that in our prosperity we shall never be moved. Thank you for making the crooked places straight! Thank you for shedding light on the dark areas and thank you for the opportunity to display your glory in every area of our life. We acknowledge that it is through you we live and move and have our being so we rest assured that You will order our steps in every area. Holy Spirit, we invite you into every decision, every obstacle, every challenge, and every part of us and that gives us peace. We also declare that the devil is defeated in every area of our lives and *Jesus is Lord In Jesus Name Amen*! *Crystal Stephens*

PRAYER OF CONDOLENCES FOR THE LOSS OF A LOVE ONE

Father GOD in the Name of Jesus. I thank you for my loved one, _____. Thank you for the time that we had together. I pray that you will help me and others to be strong as we lay our loved one _____ to rest.

I pray and believe that this is the will and plan of you Lord. But give us strength and help the family members who are having a hard time with the passing of _____. I pray that you will comfort me and them as needed. And that our family will come together in unity and love for each other even more. And I pray that you will give us all sweet reflecting moments about _____.

I pray that whatever is needed to give _____ a decent and respectful end of life service, I pray that it is so, and the finances are available.

And most of all I pray that your mercy and grace will cover _____. Continue to keep and cover us all with your love, guidance, and protection until our appointed time, to forever be in heaven with you Father GOD. These things I pray *In the Name of Jesus.*

<u>PRAYER OF CONDOLENCES</u>

I pray that it is well, and all is well with you and your family right now, Through the Blood and In the Name of Jesus. I pray that Father GOD will wrap His loving arms around you and others who are experiencing the loss of someone who was dear to you all's hearts. I pray that Father GOD will give you peace and an understanding. I pray that the sweet memories of your loved one will bring smiles and healing to the hearts as needed and at the appointed times. These things I pray, *In the Name of Jesus.*

PRAYER FOR FRIENDS

I thank you Father GOD for my friends. I thank you for allowing our paths to cross. I pray that today and always that you keep my friends safe from all hurt, harm and danger. I pray that it is well with them, their family and everything that concerns them. I pray that you will show and open the doors of pleasurable opportunities for them. I pray that it is well with them always. Continue to bless and help our friendship to grow. Help me to always be respectful, mindful of their thoughts and feelings. Thank you, Father GOD, for my friend(s).
In the Majestic Name of Your Son Jesus, Amen.

PRAYER AGAINST SUICIDE

Father GOD help me. Help me to like myself. Forgive me Lord. Help me, Lord. I need you; I need someone to help me. Thank you, GOD, thank you GOD, Thank you GOD. Lord help me. *In Jesus Name, Amen.*

PRAYER FOR SOMEONE WHO IS SUICIDAL

Lord, Psalms 107:20 says that a word can be sent to heal and deliver someone from destruction. So, Father GOD In the Name of Jesus, I'm asking that you send a word, someone, or send an angel to help _____. I know and understand that it is your power Father GOD that heals; so, I'm asking you to send a word and make things better for _____. I pray that you will take away suicidal thoughts, the pain and hurt that they are feeling right now, and let them know that everything will be okay, love on them Lord, please, love on them. As the centurion leader of the armed forces prayed for one of his soldiers to be healed, and the soldier was healed, I'm interceding and asking you to heal _____. Take away their despair and give them hope. I thank you Lord, *In the Wonderful Name of Jesus*, I pray.

PRAYER FOR THE CITY

Father GOD In the Name of Jesus, I thank you for the city. I thank you for allowing me to have a home in this city.

I pray that you will help me and my neighbors to be good stewards in our homes and surroundings. I pray that we have enough of finances to keep up our homes, yards, and anything we may need to beautify our homes and keep them in good condition.

I pray that we are helpers to one another. I pray that we and our families can safely sit on the porch, work in and enjoy our yards. And I pray that our children can safely play and walk on our blocks. _**I bind up**_ all crime and sin, and _**I loose**_, safe dwellings, peace and righteousness in this city.

I pray that we have a mayor who has integrity. I pray that all of the city officials are just and righteous. _**I bind up**_ greed and _**I loose**_ the spirit of honesty, sharing and giving in their hearts.

I pray for the churches in the city. I pray that you will give them resources, instructions, and ways to reach out to their surrounding neighborhoods and open their hearts to the needs of the community.

I pray that no one is in bondage. And if there are people who desire to come out of bondage, I intercede on their behalf and ask that you Father GOD will send a word, by any means necessary to bring them totally and permanently out of bondage. ***I bind up*** the sin and oppression that is keeping the people in bondage, and ***I loose***, the "word" of GOD and the joy of you Lord as their strength.

These things I pray, *Through the Blood and In the Name of Jesus.*

TRAVELING MERCIES PRAYER

Father GOD in The Name of Jesus, I give you glory, honor and praise. I thank you for waking me up this morning and allowing me to be in my right mind and have a smile in my heart. I thank you for having a roof over my head and grateful that I was able to dress myself.

And I thank you for not just doing those things for me but for my family and friends as well. And I decree, that no weapon formed against us shall prosper. You are so good. You've watched over us all and I'm grateful. Now Father GOD as I move forward today to another city, state, I pray that you will encamp angels all around me and keep me safe from all hurt, harm and danger, seen and unseen.

I Pray that you will be the navigator of my vehicle. (the vehicle, plane, train, bus or designated driver). I pray that you will allow me to get to my destinations safe and sound. And I pray that your peace will always be there, waiting for me. And I pray Father

GOD that I have a good fellowship and outcomes with those I encounter.

And I pray when it's time for me to go back to my home, I pray that you will encamp angels around me and again, be the navigator of my vehicle. And when I arrive home I pray your peace will be awaiting me. *These things I pray, In the Precious Name of YOUR Son Jesus.*

PRAYERS FOR HEALING AND STRENGTH

I'm touching and agreeing that you are feeling better from the healings of both Father GOD, in the spirit of Jehovah Rapha, our healer and our Lord and Saviour, Jesus, In the Name of Jesus. You are a child of the Most High GOD and I decree that no weapon formed against you shall prosper. *I bind* every ache, disease, germ, all pain, and viruses, which tries to bring discomfort to your mind, body, soul and spirit. *I loose* that those infirmities dies instantly *Through the Blood and In the Name of Jesus, and it is so.*

PRAYER OF HEALING

I speak **GOD's** blessings and healing to you and your family. No weapon formed against you or them shall prosper. I'm touching and agreeing with your faith, and desires. *Through the Blood and In the Name of Jesus, Amen and Amen.*

JUST A TOUCH FROM JESUS
PRAYING FOR OTHERS

MAY the wonderful and healing touch of Jesus, surround and shadow you. May his touch make you whole as he did for the woman who had an issue of blood for eighteen (18) years. May he make you free from all hurt, pain and infirmities. May you be healed, happy and whole. I'm touching and agreeing with you and your family for total healing in every area where there is a need. *Amen, and In the Name of Jesus.*

PRAYER FOR FEELING SAFE

I thank you GOD that your every word is pure. I thank you for being a shield and buckler to me, because I put my trust in You daily Lord. Therefore Father GOD In the Name of Jesus. I'm trusting and believing that you will keep me safe from all hurt, harm and danger, seen and unseen. And I thank you that what the enemy meant for bad, you have turn it around for my good. I'm praying that you will continue to put a shield of protection around me at all times and that no weapon formed against me shall prosper and every tongue, action and attempt that rises against me to hurt, harm and destroy me, and all that pertains to unto me and those I love, it shall be condemn. May the attempted weapons against me, boomerang on the one(s) who desired to harm me, especially to those who seek my hurt without a cause. These things I pray *In the Precious Name of Your Son, Jesus.*

PRAYER FOR CONFLICTING SITUATIONS
LOSS OF LIFE

Father GOD In the Name of Jesus, thank you. We thank you Father GOD and we know that all things are possible with you... and as You know the number of strands of hair that are on our heads, we understand that You also know our every thought and heart.

We are standing together and asking that You heal the hearts and give peace and understanding to all who are involved and affected with the loss of life. Take the anger from us all, and softly heal and guide our hearts to a place of peace, especially those who lost a loved one(s). Help us all Lord to do better. And we're praying that the person who actively caused the diminishment of someone's life be remorsefully humbled and ask You Lord for forgiveness.

We humbly ask that You forgive him/her and those who are negatively involved. We are asking for your Grace and Mercy; and that You draw him/her closer unto You and in Your will and ways, *In the Name of Jesus.*

We ask humbly that You give him/her favor with You and the Judge. We pray that no weapon formed against him/her shall prosper and that You Lord will always put a hedge of protection around him/her.

Father GOD, we know and believe that all things are possible with You and that you are a forgiving and loving GOD, thank You Father.

This we pray, Through the Blood and In the Name of Jesus, Amen and Amen

PRAYER OF ENCOURGEMENT

MAY the Joy of the Lord be your strength today and always. May Father GOD bless you and all those dear to your heart exceedingly and abundantly above all you can ever ask and think. I pray that you remain in the Joy of the Lord and continue to have a great day. Ride and walk with the joy of the Lord as your strength. And as always, I'm touching and agreeing with your faith and desires. *Amen, Through the Blood and In the Name of Jesus.*

TOUCHING AND AGREEGING PRAYER

I touch and agree that when you go forth on behalf of Father GOD to the people that you will preach, pray, walk, talk like fire is all shut up in your bones... And with the help of the Holy Ghost, you will be sound, convincing, sold out, strung out for the LORD, and to the Kingdom of GOD. And I pray as you continue to go forth, In the Name of Jesus that the Lord will help, teach and show you the hearts and needs of the congregation. So, In the Name of Jesus go forth, and praise Father GOD for you being sound and whole in Christ Jesus. *It is Through the Blood and In the Name of Jesus, that it shall be so, and all is well, Amen.*

PRAYER FOR OTHERS
ORDERED STEPS

I pray that the Lord will order your steps to something beautiful and perfectly timed for you. I pray that Father GOD will grant you the desires of your heart. I pray that he will always keep you from all hurt, harm and danger, seen and unseen. I pray that Father GOD will always put a hedge of protection around you. I pray that you will know your purpose in life and that you're on the right path. I pray that the Lord will give you a seasonal word of hope for yourself and others as needed, especially for people who are searching for something more and better. And I pray you have located your niche, and everything is in divine order and timed just for you. May Father GOD bless you now and always, Glory to Father GOD, *In the Precious Name of Jesus.*

<u>WELCOME PRAYER</u>
JOINT FELLOWSHIP CONGREGATION

Greetings in the Majestic Name of our Saviour Christ Jesus. We pray that all is well with everyone this very moment. We're glad and delighted that you desire to fellowship with us on this special and glorious day. For this is the day that the Lord has made and we shall rejoice and be glad in it. We are excited about the message that the Lord will be sending to us all. May it refresh, encourage and bless our hearts tremendously. Get comfortable, be relaxed and may GOD's grace and peace be with you now and always. And again, welcome, we are joyful that you are here with us today. *In Jesus Name, Amen.*

BENEDICTION PRAYER

I thank you Father GOD for this gathering. I pray that everyone has felt your presence and received what you have predestined and ordained just for them. For your word says that you knew us in the womb. I pray that the leaders of the set gathering will be refilled, restored, energized with new revelation knowledge, encouragement, and hope from you O'LORD.

May you order our steps daily; may you always go before us and open the doors that need to be opened and shut the doors, put a lock on the doors that we don't need to enter. And may you bless each and every one of us with traveling mercies, as we leave this meeting and through the upcoming days. And when we arrive at our homes may your angels of protection, guide us into our homes. And may your love and peace sustain us always. *These things we pray in The Majestic Name of Your Son, Christ Jesus, our Saviour, Amen.*

BENEDICTION PRAYER
And Blessed Establishment

Father GOD In the Name of Jesus. We thank you for showing up in the power of the Holy Ghost. We thank you that everything was done decently and in order. Now that we're leaving this place, establishment, we pray that you will cover us and keep our minds stead on you until will meet and come together again.

We love You Father GOD, Lord Jesus, and the Holy Spirit, thank you. Now bless this dwelling location also. Keep it tidy, pretty and comfortable for the dwelling of your people. We pray that if there is any part of this dwelling location that is in need of an uplifting, we pray that you will show us where and provide us with the necessary resources to make it happen. We thank you Father, *In the Precious Name of Your Only Begotten Son, Jesus, our Saviour, hope, and redeemer*. Thank You Lord.

CHAPTER 8 EIGHT

TOTALLY TRUSTING GOD

It is good to exhaust all of GOD's remedies from the bible, what He personally tells us and what we've read about before giving in to a suggestion or idea that we're not sure about. When we try to make a situation better from the examples and what the "word" of GOD says from the bible; and we still have a negative outcome, then we can occasionally assume that the awkwardness and discomfort is of GOD; and that He has a purpose for allowing the situation to happen, because He's a GOD of purpose. *Ecclesiastes 3:1, Isaiah 14:24-27, and Romans 8:28.*

The discomfort could be a test from GOD. GOD seeing if we totally trust Him, so that He can bless us even the more; an Abraham and his son, Isaac test, *Genesis 22:11.* It could also be a test for GOD to know if we've been listening to Him and following His instructions. Like Adam, GOD created the animals, but He told Adam to name them, and Adam did. Because tests and trials come to make us patient, strong and let us know what were capable of accomplishing, *James 1:2* and *1 Peter 1:7*. And if it's one of the latter two, be assured that we're not being made patient and strong for ourselves only, but for others too. It's a testimony that will give us all hope as to how an uncomfortable predicament could possibly end. And help us learn and know where our faith is and how much we truly believe in, as well as trust GOD. GOD also desires that we draw closer to Him, so He demonstrates to us how faithful His "word" is by allowing something we prayed for to come to fruition, something that we can't make happen nor get the credit for, but GOD can, and GOD will.

There are lots of people, some attend church and some are unchurched who haven't trusted GOD totally. Total trust in GOD is a benefit, on the road that will cause us to have a reasonable happy, wellbeing and productive life.

When we're physically down and things are not up to par, we seek a doctor, or we sometimes intoxicate ourselves with booze, pills, drugs, and we listen to other people's advice, who don't always have our best interest before seeking GOD. Seeking some of the world's answers or leaning to our own understandings regarding matters, can cost us dearly, make things more miserable than how they previously began. All because we didn't totally trust GOD and exhaust His remedies first, which are financially free of charge. Reading his" word", following his instructions and having faith will cause us to know, with an understanding about His remedies. Remedies, such as prayer, bind and loose principles, affirmations, confessions and having the right people to intercede for us *(confessing our faults to one another)*.

There's a scripture in the bible, *2 Chronicles 16:12-14* that tells us how GOD allowed a king's life to end, because he didn't consult GOD first with his illness, and *(he probably should've have known better)*. And there's another scripture *Luke 8:43* where a woman had an issue of blood for twelve years, spent all the money she had on that illness and was still sick. It wasn't until she heard about Jesus and what he could do that she become healed and whole. She believed what she had heard *(possibly read as well)* about Jesus. When an opportunity came for her to be in his presence, she pressed her way towards Jesus, touched the hem of his garment and she immediately became whole, healed.

Getting to the root of matters, by seeking GOD's various ways to being healed, healthy and whole in every aspect of our lives, is key, if we desire to have a less or be free from certain physical infirmities, lack of finances, low self-esteem, and unhealthy relationships.

Becoming proactive about issues that concern us will keep negative things from happening to us and the rightful things will linger and surround us. We should regularly or as much as possible, implement, the bind and loose principles, say affirmations, confessions, confess our faults to one another, as it says in *James 5:16* and pray to Father GOD. Those acts of faith will leave us with results, that will cause us to become healed, healthy, and whole as needed. The bible also says to pray without ceasing, *1 Thessalonians 5:17,* which means, always.

Speaking our desires and bringing them into existence by saying something will put us on the path of success and lead us to our purposes in life. Because after all, Jesus says in *John 10:10*, that he came that we may have life, and life more abundantly and not just an average life, nor what society says we should have, but more than the norm, above average kind of life.

Whether we're, saying affirmations, using the bind and loose principles, praying to Father GOD, interceding on the behalf of someone else or confessing our faults to one another, one thing is for sure, they all need a voice to make them happen; someone will need to **say** something for victory to occur.

CHAPTER 9 NINE

SCRIPTURES AND BIBLE STORIES

To motivate, inspire and nudge someone to go hard after the things pertaining to the Kingdom of GOD; to Encourage and Increase One's Faith. And study to show thyself approved.

Scriptures that you can pray for yourself and others.

Hear this, all ye people; give ear, all ye inhabitants of the world: Both low and high, rich and poor, together. **My mouth shall speak of wisdom**; and the meditation of my heart shall be of understanding.

Psalms 49:1-3

THE BENEFITS OF PRAYING
FROM THE HEART
James 5:13-18

Is any among you afflicted? **let him pray**. Is any merry? let him sing psalms. Is any sick among you? let him call for the elders of the church; and let them pray over him, anointing him with oil in the name of the Lord. And **the prayer of faith** shall save the sick, and the Lord shall raise him up and if he have committed sins, they shall be forgiven him. Confess your faults one to another, and pray one for another, that ye may be healed. The **effectual prayers of a righteous man availeth much**. Elias was a man subject to like passions as we are, and he **prayed earnestly** that it might not rain: and it rained not on the earth by the space of three years and six months. And he **prayed again**, and the heaven gave rain, and the earth brought forth her fruit.

A KING WHO DESIRED TO TREAT PEOPLE WITH RIGHTEOUSNESS AND RESPECT
2 Chronicles 1:7-12

In that night did GOD appear unto Solomon, and said unto him, Ask What I shall give thee. And Solomon said unto GOD, Thou hast shewed great mercy unto David my father; and hast made me to reign in his stead. Now, O LORD GOD, let thy promise unto David my father be established: for thou has made me king over a people like the dust of the earth in multitude. Give me now wisdom and knowledge, that I may go out and come in before this people: for who can judge this thy people, that is so great: And GOD said to Solomon, Because this was in thine heart, and thou **hast not asked** riches, wealth, or honour, nor the life of thine enemies, neither yet had asked long life; but **hast asked** wisdom and knowledge for thyself, that thou mayest judge my people, over whom I have made thee king. Wisdom and knowledge is granted unto thee; and I will give thee riches, and wealth, and honour, such as none of the kings have had that been before thee, neither shall there any after thee have the like.

<u>2 Chronicles 7:11-15</u>

Thus Solomon, finished the house of the LORD, and the king's house: and all that came into Solomon's heart to make in the house of the LORD, and in his own house, prosperously effected. And the LORD appeared to Solomon by night, and said unto him, I have **heard thy prayer**, and have chosen this place to myself for a house of sacrifice. If I shut up heaven that there be nor rain, or if I command the locusts to devour the land, or if I send pestilence among my people; If my people, which are called by my name, shall humble themselves, and **pray and seek my face**, and turn from their wicked ways; then will I hear from heaven, and will forgive their sin, and will heal their land. Now mine eyes shall be open, and **mine ears attent unto the prayer that is made in this place**.

A HUMBLED PRAYER FROM SOMEONE WHO KNEW AND UNDERSTOOD THEIR SHORTCOMINGS AND THAT THEY NEEDED GOD
Psalms 141

LORD, I cry unto thee: make haste unto me; give ear unto my voice, when I cry unto thee. **Let my prayer be set forth before thee as incense; and the lifting up of my hands as the evening sacrifice.** Set a watch, O LORD, before my mouth; keep the door of my lips. Incline not my heart to *any* evil thing, to practise wicked works with men that work iniquity: and let me not eat of their dainties. Let the righteous smite me; it shall be a kindness: and let him reprove me; it shall be an excellent oil, which shall not break my head: for yet **my prayer** also shall be in their calamities. When their judges are overthrown in stony places, they shall hear my words; for they are sweet.

And he saw that there was no man, and wondered that there was no intercessor: therefore his arm brought salvation unto him; and his righteousness, it sustained him. For he put on righteousness as a breastplate, and an helmet of salvation upon his head; and he put on the garments of vengeance for clothing, and was clad with zeal as a cloke. According to their deeds, accordingly he will repay, fury to his adversaries, recompence to his enemies; to the islands he will repay recompence. So shall they fear the name of the LORD from the west, and his glory from the rising of the sun. When the enemy shall come in like a flood, the Spirit of the LORD shall lift up a standard against him. And the Redeemer shall come to Zion, and unto them that turn from transgression in Jacob, saith the LORD. **As for me, this is my covenant with them, saith the LORD; My spirit that is upon thee, and my words which I have put in thy mouth, shall**

not depart out of thy mouth, nor out of the mouth of thy seed, nor out of the mouth of thy seed's seed, saith the LORD, from henceforth and for ever.

WHAT GOD DOES FOR THOSE HE HAS CHOSEN
Jeremiah 1:4-12

Then the word of the LORD came unto me, saying, Before I formed thee in the belly I knew thee; and before thou camest forth out of the womb I sanctified thee, and I ordained thee a prophet unto the nations. **Then said I, Ah, Lord GOD! behold, I cannot speak**: for I am a child. But **the LORD said** unto me, **Say not, I *am* a child: for thou shalt go to all that I shall send thee, and whatsoever I command thee thou shalt speak.** Be not afraid of their faces: for I *am* with thee to deliver thee, saith the LORD. **Then the LORD put forth his hand, and touched my mouth.** And the LORD said unto me, Behold, **I have put my words in**

thy mouth. See, I have this day set thee over the nations and over the kingdoms, to root out, and to pull down, and to destroy, and to throw down, to build, and to plant. Moreover the word of the LORD came unto me, saying, Jeremiah, what seest thou? And I said a rod of an almond tree. **Then said the LORD unto me, Thou hast well seen: for I will hasten my word to perform it.**

BENEFITS THAT COVERS YOUR TOTAL WELL BEING
Psalms 103:1-22

Bless the LORD, O my soul: and all that is within me, bless his holy name. Bless the LORD, O my soul, and forget not all his benefits: **Who forgiveth all thine iniquities; Who healeth all thy diseases; Who redeemeth thy life from destruction; Who crowneth thee with lovingkindness and tender mercies; Who satisfieth thy mouth** with good things; so that thy youth is renewed like the eagle's. The LORD executeth righteousness and judgment for all that are oppressed. He made known his ways unto Moses, his acts unto the children of Israel. The LORD is merciful and gracious, slow to anger, and plenteous in mercy.

PRAYER OF THANKS
Luke 18:9-14

The Prayers from two men, a Pharisee and a Publican. The Pharisee was proud and thought he was perfect; and the Publican was grateful, aware of his issues and knew that he wasn't always pleasing to himself and GOD.

And he spake this parable unto certain which trusted in themselves that they were righteous, and despised others: Two men went up into the temple to pray; the one a Pharisee, and the other a publican. The Pharisee stood and prayed thus with himself, GOD, I thank thee, that I am not as other men are, extortioners, unjust, adulterers, or even as this publican. I fast twice in the week, I give tithes of all that I possess. **And the**

publican, standing afar off, would not lift up so much as his eyes unto heaven, but smote upon his breast, saying, GOD be merciful to me a sinner. I tell you, this man went down to his house justified rather than the other: for every one that exalteth himself shall be abased; and he that humbleth himself shall be exalted.

BIBLE STORY AND
WORDS OF INHIERTENCE BLESSINGS
Genesis 27:24-30

When Isaac Blessed Jacob with an inheritance he said and had actions following his words. He didn't bless Jacob by leaving him a bunch of material things, but Isaac, Jacob's dad blessed Jacob with his words, which empowered Jacob to reach, acquire and have, all the blessings that he would need to be powerfully wise and wealthy like his dad Isaac.

BIBLE STORY AND
PRAYER OF SUPPLICATION
1 Samuel 1:1-28
Petitioning to GOD for a Miracle to Give Birth

Hannah was a wife who was barren, no children, but was honest, righteous and loved GOD. She prayed to GOD for a child. She prayed so hard to GOD (*mentally and verbally*) that people thought she was drunk. And GOD indeed granted Hannah her prayer, a child whom she named Samuel.

BIBLE STORY AND
HEZEKIAH SICKNESS AND
GENUINE PRAYER UNTO GOD
Isaiah 38:1-8

The Prophet went to Hezekiah and told him to get his life in order because he was about to die. Because Hezekiah knew and had a relationship with GOD he was able to wholeheartedly pray unto Father GOD, asking Him to change His mind. GOD did change his mind and added fifteen additional years to Hezekiah's life.

BIBLE STORY AND
PRAYER OF SUPPLICATION AN INTERCESSION
Jeremiah 42:1-12

Believing who GOD is and what He can and will do; Being humbled, honest and believing GOD's Prophets, compelled, captains, children of kings, and a community to repent before GOD and ask the Prophet Jeremiah to go before GOD for them (intercede through prayer). Jeremiah the Prophet interceded on their behalf. And GOD saved, and delivered them from the hands of a ruthless King in Babylon. GOD gave them love, grace, mercy and allowed them to get back to their own land.

BIBLE STORY AND PRAYER OF SUPPLICATION
Daniel 9:3-4 and Daniel 9:17-23

Making Your Request Known

Daniel knowing and believing that GOD's "word" is true, and He keeps His promises. Daniel confessed his sins and the sins of the people before GOD. And GOD immediately took notice, and attentively answered the prayers of those who loved, were sold out and obedient to Him.

BIBLE STORY AND DELAYED, BUT ANSWERED PRAYER

Daniel 10:1-12

Daniel was mourning and not sure if his prayers were going to be answered, because a few weeks had passed by, and his circumstances hadn't changed. But not giving up, having faith and being steadfast to the things of GOD, caused Daniel to be assured by a vision that his (your) prayers were heard and will be answered according to his (your) desires.

BIBLE STORY OF BEING BLESSED
AND CHOSEN
WORDS OF ADORATION
Luke 1:26-49

After Mary, the mother of Jesus received a visit (message) from Gabriel, an Angel sent by GOD telling her that she was chosen by GOD to be the carrier of the Holy Child, our Saviour, Redeemer, Christ Jesus, she went to see her cousin Elizabeth, (John the Baptist, mother). And what was told to her by Gabriel the Angel, was also confirmed to her by her cousin Elizabeth. Mary praised, worshipped, and adored GOD, for choosing her. It was a prayer of belief, adoration and thanks towards GOD.

BIBLE STORY AND PRAYER OF INTERCESSION
(CORPORATE)
John 14:8-21

Jesus was hoping that his disciples believed in his works and who he was, the Messiah, Saviour, Reedemer of the World. And prayed to GOD for them, that GOD would send them help, the Comforter after he, (Jesus) completed his assignment on Earth and went back to Heaven.

VARIOUS NAMES
OF GOD

AND

TYPES OF PRAYERS

NAMES of GOD

Whatever you're praying about that's the GOD whom you can ask; if you desire to be personable with Father GOD.

Abba, Father, Jehovah
Mark 14:36   Romans 8:15   Galatians 4:6

Alpha and Omega, The Beginning and End
Revelation 1:8; 1:11; 21:6; 22:13

Adonai
Lord, Master over Everything

El Olam
The Everlasting GOD
Genesis 21:33

El Roi
The GOD Who Sees

El Elyon
The Most High GOD

Elohim

GOD is Creator

El Shaddai

Lord God Almighty, More than Enough

Jehovah

GOD Almighty   Exodus 6:3

The Most High GOD   Psalms 83:18

GOD is my Strength   Isaiah 12:2

Everlasting Strength   Isaiah 26:4

Jehovah GHMOLAH

The GOD Who Recompense

Isaiah 65:6; Ezekiel 9:10; 17:19

2 Thessalonians 1:6;   Hebrews 10:30

Jehovah JIREH

The Lord Will Provide   Genesis 22:13

Jehovah MACCADDESHEM

The Lord Who Sanctifies

Exodus 29:44; Leviticus 21:15; 21:23; 22:9; 22:16;

Isaiah 29:23; Ezekiel 37:28

Jehovah ROHI
The Lord My Shepherd   Psalm 23:1

Jehovah RAPHA
The Lord Our Healer   Exodus 15:26

Jehovah SABBAOTH
The Lord of Hosts

Jehovah SHALOM
The Lord is Peace   Judges 6:24

Jehovah SHAMMAH
The Lord is There

Jehovah NISSI
The Lord our Banner   Exodus 17:8

Jehovah TSIDKENU
The Lord our Righteousness

YAHWEH
Lord, Jehovah

TYPES OF PRAYERS

Adoration

- Your feelings towards Father GOD; to pray at all times. Devoted love and admiration. Worship (adore: love and admire very greatly.)

Affirm & Affirmations:

- Declare positively to be true. Maintain firmly
- A positive statement; assertion a solemn declaration having the legal force of an oath and made by persons whose religion or conscience forbids the taking of an oath. Confirmation or ratification.
- Stating that a fact is so; answering yes to a question put or implied.

Benediction:

- Prayed at the end of a meeting or church service. The asking of GOD's blessing, at the end of a church service or a marriage ceremony. The form or ritual of this invocation. Blessing.

Confessions:

- An owning up; acknowledgement; admission. Admission of guilt. The telling of one's sins to a priest in the sacrament of penance or

reconciliation in order to obtain forgiveness.
Things confessed. Acknowledgment of belief;
profession of faith. Belief acknowledged. Creed.
Confessor: person who confesses. A person
who verbally acknowledges belief.

Warfare: Binding & loosing

- Armed conflict; war; fighting. And struggle or
  contest. (war: strife)

Decree:

- Something ordered or settled by authority;
  official decision. A decision or order of a court
  or judge. Law of a church council, especially
  one settling a disputed point of doctrine. Order
  or settle by authority. Decide, determine.

Intercession Intercessor, Intercede:

- Plead for another; ask a favor from one person
  for another. Act as an intermediary in order to
  bring about an agreement; mediate. Go
  between. Act or fact of interceding. Prayer
  pleading for others.

Supplication:

- Beg, humbly and earnestly. Pray humbly. A
  humble prayer addressed to GOD or a deity.

Thanks & Thanksgiving:

- Act of thanking; expression of gratitude and pleasure. Feeling of kindness received; gratitude. A giving of thanks. Expression of thanks. Telling GOD thank you, just because, at your leisure.

Welcome:

- Pray at the beginning of a gathering or service. Greet kindly; give a friendly reception too. Receive gladly. A kind reception. Gladly received, gladly or freely permitted. Free to enjoy courtesies without obligation. Exclamation of friendly greeting.

End each prayer, with either of the following three:

"In the Name of Jesus"

or

"Through the Blood and In the Name of Jesus"

or

"Sealed in the Name and Blood of Jesus"

CHAPTER 11 ELEVEN

CONCLUSION

Saying confessions, affirmations, and prayers on a regular basis, will cause us to have fewer negative encounters and situations in our space, and on our paths. They will also change our thought process, elevate our faith, and increase our vocabulary to a new, better way of thinking and living.

We are going to say something, so why not say the right words and create conversations that result in positive situations as well as possibilities. If you don't' have a lot of GOD's **"word"** in you, say what you know, and GOD will honor your faith.

The environment we're surrounded by and the people who we choose to associate ourselves with will frequently determine how we feel and the words we say. People who are happy and content produce positive conversations with rewarding outcomes. People who complain and look for fault in others produce negative conversations that usually evolves into negative situations.

Adding fruitful words and conversations into our atmosphere, the way we routinely incorporate meals into our daily lives is a benchmark to strive for. Because the enemy *(those who lie and do negative hateful things)* is busy trying to trap us, discourage us, prohibit our faith, hope, and goals by the words he hears us say as well as other means too. Remember, *Proverbs 18:21* says, "life and death are in the power of the tongue".

Even though the enemy is busy, one thing is for sure, GOD is more powerful than the enemy, and GOD's **"word"** and principles does not come back void. They are sharper than any two-edged sword, precise and changes not. GOD's **"word"** is truth, life, and love. *"Heaven and earth shall pass away, but my <u>words</u> shall not pass away".* *Matthew 24:35*

Let us not put limits on GOD because of the things we say. The **"word"** says that all things are possible if we believe in GOD. Concentrate on giving your best efforts daily towards living and trusting how Jesus,

GOD's Only Begotten Son, says man (we) should live, *(Matthew – Acts & Revelations)*.

Each of us uniquely represents a part of GOD's image. GOD has created us with our own personal desires and intimate ways of being connected to Him through His **"word"**. Let's not insult nor be unappreciative towards GOD, by looking at others. We need to appreciate who and how He has created us to be. GOD doesn't error; we are wonderfully and fearfully made.

Being sensitive, having attentive ears and saying the right words will uplift our posture, change our location to a place in life where there will be no more excuses, lack of knowledge, and reasons why we don't have enough of the needful as well as the meaningful things of life in our grasp.

Being open to learn, know, and understand more about the **"word"** of GOD along with His methodology, will increase our faith. Our faith will mature and become unwavering, a solid concrete foundation, in a joyful spacious atmosphere, because we're now saying the right words as well as doing the right things. *"And Jesus looking upon them saith, With men it is impossible, but not with GOD: for with GOD all things are possible."* Mark 10:27

Teach me, and I will hold my tongue: and cause me to understand wherein I have erred, how <u>forcible</u> are the right words. Job 6:24-25

And from the days of John the Baptist until now the Kingdom of heaven suffereth violence, and the violent take it by <u>force</u>. Matthew 11:12

And the apostles said unto the Lord, Increase our faith. And the Lord said, If ye had faith as a grain of mustard seed, ye might say unto this sycamine tree, Be thou plucked up by the root, and be thou planted in the sea; and it should obey you. Luke 17:5

How sweet are thy words unto my taste! Yea, sweeter than honey to my mouth! Psalms 119:103

Brenda J. Mills is a public service retiree. She worked in the public-school setting for more than thirty years in the capacity of a noon hour aide, secretary, certified K-8, All Subjects Teacher and as a McKinney Vento Homeless Liaison.

Brenda has more than seventeen years of experience as a biblical youth teacher, and annually supported Vacation Bible School for more than fifteen years, with five of those years as the director of VBS. And for more than seven years she worked during the summer months with children in the neighborhood at Monteith Presbyterian Church, *(the late Raymond Lumley, was Pastor)*. The summer youth program for ages four-sixteen was called "Alphabet Soup".

The author's religious and bible foundation began at First Baptist World Changers International Ministries, Detroit, Michigan under the guidance and watch care of *Apostle Dr. Lennell. D. Caldwell and Pastor Dr. Carol. D. Caldwell.*

This book *"Speak, SAY, Pray"*, is Brenda's sixth authored book. Brenda considers herself to be a creative writer which complements and goes along perfectly with her other skills, as a dressmaker, fabric re-constructor, home decorator, and artist.

Brenda and her husband Tony L. Mills, Sr., are parents of a blended family which comprises five adult children and thirteen (ten plus three) grandchildren.

OTHER BOOKS WRITTEN BY *Brenda*

"The Children's Bread"
(12-Months "Christian Curriculum")

"The Children's Bread (2)"
(Fundamental Biblical Information Especially for New Christians and Biblical Teachers)

"The "Children's Bread for Toddlers"
(Colorful Monthly Lessons and Academically Written)

"(26) Ways (78) Reasons Don't Give Up"
(Scriptural Based and Creatively Written Utilizing the Alphabet)

"The Power of GOD is Christ Jesus, The True Essence of Power"
(Where to Find Real Power to Do All Things)